Anonymous

Progress and Prospects of New York,

the first city of the world. 1492-1893

Anonymous

Progress and Prospects of New York,
the first city of the world. 1492-1893

ISBN/EAN: 9783337425944

Printed in Europe, USA, Canada, Australia, Japan

Cover: Foto ©Suzi / pixelio.de

More available books at **www.hansebooks.com**

PROGRESS AND PROSPECTS

OF

NEW YORK

THE FIRST CITY OF THE WORLD.

1492—1893.

PUBLISHED BY THE

COMMERCIAL TRAVELERS CLUB,
OF NEW YORK CITY.
1893.

IN COMPILING THE PAGES OF THIS
SOUVENIR BOOK, IT HAS BEEN OUR PUR-
POSE TO ISSUE A PUBLICATION WORTHY,
IN ALL RESPECTS, OF THE ORGANIZATION
WHICH IT TYPIFIES. THE GREATEST RE-
WARD WHICH WE CAN RECEIVE FOR OUR
HUMBLE BUT EARNEST SERVICES IS THE
KNOWLEDGE THAT OUR WORK HAS MET
WITH THE APPROVAL OF THE PRESS, OUR
BROTHER COMMERCIAL TRAVELERS, AND
FRIENDS.

A. S. WILLDIGG,
G. W. PROCTOR KNOTT,
JOHN G. HART,
SOUVENIR COMMITTEE.
COMMERCIAL TRAVELERS CLUB. NEW YORK.

To the

Merchants, Manufacturers and Bankers,

THROUGH whose energy and progressive ability the City of New York has been advanced to the foremost place among the great commercial and industrial centers of the world; whose enterprise and liberality have adorned it with palatial mercantile establishments, great factories, immense warehouses, magnificent parks, benevolent institutions and residences; and whose unimpaired integrity has imparted a world-wide financial credit to the city, is this publication respectfully inscribed by the

COMMERCIAL TRAVELERS' CLUB.

RAILROAD FREIGHT AND PASSENGER AGENTS' DINNER,

THE "ARENA," 41 WEST THIRTY-FIRST STREET,

FEBRUARY 14, 1893.

NEW YORK, February 18, 1893.

MR. GEORGE W. PROCTOR KNOTT,

President Commercial Travelers Club, New York City.

DEAR MR. KNOTT: When Mr. H. W. Dearborn, Chairman of your Railroad Committee, waited upon members of our committee and very kindly tendered the hospitalities and use of the Commercial Travelers Club House for a "quiet smoke," after our dinner on Tuesday last, we had not the slightest idea of what was in store for us.

We had supposed up to the time of leaving our dinner table that nothing better could be had, but a few moments in your lovely home showed that the pleasures of our evening had only just begun.

Our guests for that occasion were representative Railroad men from the sister cities of Boston and Philadelphia, and we numbered all told about 105.

Your representative at our dinner invited "every mother's son" of us, and insisted upon all accompanying him to "No. 15 this street, boys—a few doors below."

It is needless to tell you they went, for your records must show.

How can we ever thank the C. T. Club for the generous hospitality they extended?

How can we ever thank you for sitting up so late with us?

How can we ever thank your Mr. W. A. Power for the lovely music he discoursed the whole time and never seemed to tire in the least?

We do not feel that we owe you any apology for staying as late as we did, for we think it was the fault of your members. They simply refused to let us go.

On behalf of those who were there, we desire to extend to your Club our most sincere thanks for the happy time you gave us and our guests, and assure you it is impressed so indelibly in the minds of every one present that it will never be forgotten.

We trust the occasion may present itself when we can, in part at least, repay the compliment you so happily extended us, and wish for your Club the prosperity and success it so justly deserves.

With much regard, we are, very truly yours,

A. H. PAINE, Chicago and Northwestern ;

M. C. ROACH, New York Central and Hudson River ;

W. J. BOGERT, Chicago and Alton ;

R. TENBROECK, Union Pacific ;

GEO. R. FITCH, Northern Pacific ;

C. D. SIMONSON, Atchison, Topeka and Santa Fe ;

H. B. McCLELLAN, Wabash ;

M. G. VANDERGAW, Pennsylvania ;

F. L. MANCHESTER, Missouri, Kansas and Texas ;

T. J. KLASE, Reading System ;

H. B. JAGOE, West Shore ;

A. B. FARNSWORTH, Chicago, Rock Island and Pacific ;

PER WM. J. BOGERT.

ROLL OF HONOR.

INDEX TO SUBSCRIBERS.

CLASSIFIED INDEX TO ADVERTISERS.

NEW YORK AND THE COMMERCIAL TRAVELER.

FOR all useful, benevolent, and legislative purposes, organization in the forms of social and civil combinations is the only force that can achieve practical and beneficial results. It is the establishment of power and the means through which it is wisely or oppressively exercised.

Capital is organized to carry forward useful enterprises. Labor is organized for mutual benefits and protection. Churches are organized to uphold and advance their teachings. Special departments of skilled industry are organized that an influence may be exerted beyond the power of individual effort. Every instrument of society, every organization, every school, every bank, must be like a well-equipped machine, in order to run smoothly and successfully.

The merchant and the commercial traveler should share alike the benefits of organization. The vast machinery of trade that has covered the continent with gleaming rails, and whitened the seas with great ships, and built cities where millions of artisans and weavers, mechanics and builders, in a thousand industries are busy in the production of goods for distribution, has made it possible to amass colossal fortunes, and spread the streams of wealth over the nation. In this amazing progress the commercial traveler has been an important factor. Is it unwise to predict that New York City will, within twenty years, at the present rate of increase, surpass London with a life-time of twenty centuries, and become the capital of the world in wealth and population? If one may judge by past progress this statement is a safe one, especially when it is known that New York's growth is based upon the rapid but permanent development of natural conditions more favorable than those that surround any other city of the world. When abroad, the New Yorker modestly speaks of "The Metropolis," because he feels that its preeminence is beyond question. New York's greatest advertisement is through that class of hard-working, active, tireless, enterprising, and aggressive men known as commercial travelers, and it is eminently proper that the value and great importance of their services should be recognized by the business community in a fitting manner.

New York, with its rail and water lines stretching forth their feeders and feeders, placing the products of the farm, forest, factory, and the mine at our very doors, has reached the limit of expansion in regard to its routes of travel. It must now compete with other distributing centers in the hot contest for preeminence, and it remains for the traveler, under these conditions, to secure the full complement of trade and commerce that will eventually crown this island as the richest spot of ground on the globe, adorned with art, surfeited with luxury, and groaning under billions of wealth.—R. B. F.

HON. WILLIAM SCHWARZWAELDER

WILLIAM SCHWARZWAELDER.

R. WILLIAM SCHWARZWAELDER was born in Baden, Germany, sixty-one years ago, but he crossed the Atlantic in company with his parents, when only five months old, in a sailing ship. He received his education in the public schools of New York City, where his parents located, and where they resided until 1850, when they removed to Brooklyn. He has been a resident of the City of Churches ever since, where he has been an honored and respected citizen. For fully five years he was a member of the Board of Education of that city, and while other public offices have been tendered him, including a nomination for the Mayoralty, and Commissioner of Public Works, he has invariably declined all public recognition.

The house of William Schwarzwaelder & Co. was originally established in 1834 by the brother of the gentleman who is now at the head of the firm. When William entered the employ of his brother at the age of fourteen, there were three stores under the management of the firm, one of which was at No. 9 East Broadway, and which continued in operation for forty-seven years; another at 109 Fulton Street, and a third in the City of Philadelphia. Mr. William Schwarzwaelder went into partnership with his brother in 1858, the style of the firm being C. Schwarzwaelder & Bro. In 1870 William became the sole proprietor, and so continued until 1879, since which time it has been William Schwarzwaelder & Co.

The house of Schwarzwaelder & Co. was for a long time the pioneer in the export furniture trade, doing the bulk of the business transacted in that line in this city. Later, however, the firm drifted into special order work, manufacturing office furniture, including desks, chairs, and all the paraphernalia that go to make up a complete office outfit for the leading banking houses, insurance companies, railroads, and other similar corporations. For years past they have supplied most of the railroad companies having offices in this city with their outfits. The house does more business in this line than all other establishments in the city put together. It carries at all times in stock from two to three thousand desks for immediate delivery, and can turn out as many as six hundred desks per month. Its capacity for chairs is equal to six hundred per day. The factory for the manufacture of desks and other cabinet work is located at Whitesboro, on the New York Central Railroad, while its chair factory is in the Catskill Mountains, where the firm owns 5,000 acres of virgin timber land.

The measure of the value of the assistance furnished often depends largely upon the emergency of the situation; or, to use a homely adage, "A friend in need is a friend indeed." It was Mr. William Schwarzwaelder who proved the true friend of the Commercial Travelers' Club, just at the time when such friendship was most needed. A Trustee was in demand whose reputation was above reproach, and whose position in the commercial world was second to none. Mr. Schwarzwaelder graciously accepted the office, which he has filled to the entire satisfaction of all parties interested.

EXTERIOR NEW COMMERCIAL TRAVELERS CLUB.
18 West Thirty first Street New York City.

THE COMMERCIAL TRAVELER AND THE CLUB.

" As we journey through life,
Let us live by the way."

TRAVELERS who are club *habitués* have "a superior cut." Their manners are more courtly, and they have cultivated, if not a higher order of intelligence, certainly a show of it. They charge for both in their sales, and rightly. In the present era of social and political combinations the club puts the seller and the purchaser on an equal footing, and tends to the maintenance of prices.

In the Travelers' Club of London, organized in 1814, "no person is considered eligible who has not traveled out of the British Islands to a distance of at least five hundred miles from London in a direct line." That distance in those days would equal a transcontinental trip now. "The committee are empowered to invite foreigners of distinction to the club, as visitors for six months; they can also invite as visitors, for one month at a time, British travelers whose usual place of residence is at a distance from the metropolis."

This is the example we have followed in extending the privileges of the Commercial Travelers Club of New York to members of all other clubs. Of course, in the substantial form of the Travelers League the ruling or supreme power is vested in the National Committee of the League Clubs. At all the clubs once a month the commercial travelers and head-pushers in all lines meet and confer together. The best clubs are those where men of commerce, professional men, and men of the world commune together.

The club tends to keep alive sympathies which might otherwise be lost; and as a bond of union, it is scarcely too much to say that clubs preserve much of that virtue of the early chivalry in its cosmopolitan features. Then, added to these, it will be the proper thing for the National League of Travelers Clubs to have a summer retreat, where the weary and dust-laden traveler can sojourn by the ever-sounding sea; where it will be allowable for married members to take their wives, to dine amidst refined surroundings along with admirably trained servants.

On the tables of the reception-room of the New York Club are found the New York daily papers; also the leading dailies of Chicago, Boston, and other cities, together with the "monthlies" and the illustrated "weeklies," which make it a pleasant place to pass an idle hour.

One of the social features of the club are fortnightly "Smokers," given by the musical members of the club and their friends. From two to three hundred are usually present, and at the close of the programme a lunch is served by the club caterer.

RECEPTION AND SMOKING ROOMS, COMMERCIAL TRAVELERS CLUB.

15 West Thirty-first Street, New York City

Members of the Commercial Travelers Club, as they travel about, issue to their customers who contemplate visiting New York City the following card of entertainment :

Commercial Travelers Club

15 WEST 31st STREET NEW YORK

The Freedom of the Club House
is extended to

Mr

for   Days from   189

Member.

On presentation of this card the bearer receives the honorary extension of the privileges of the club house.—R. B. F.

COMMERCIAL TRAVELERS CLUB OF NEW YORK.

HE Commercial Traveler is essentially a social being; deprived for the greater part of the time of the comforts of a home and the society of those dearest to him, he turns instinctively to the companionship of his fellow-man wherever found; he hails the appearance of a brother traveler as one caravan hails another in the trackless Sahara. When there are no acquaintances at hand, he makes them, in fact, he is constantly adding to his store of friends. He scatters them along the path of his pilgrimage, and his thoughts are brightened by the knowledge that cordial welcomes from friendly lips await him on his return. Sociability is a part of his organization; it is the Golden Rule of his creed; it is the corner stone of his success. Animated by this idea, the nomads of trade, the wandering heralds of commerce, naturally turn toward the comforts of the Club. Some idea of these comforts may be gained from the illustration which shows the cozy parlors, and gives a glimpse of the anterooms of the Commercial Travelers Club of New York; but, of course, it cannot reproduce the color harmony of the decorations, or the atmosphere of good fellowship which pervades the place.

The Commercial Travelers Club of New York is the outgrowth of Fraternity for the Mutual Protection and Benefit of the Members of the Club and of all Commercial Travelers. In the summer of 1894, the Commercial Travelers Club of New York came into existence. It was warmly greeted. Its establishment was soon made known by that swift Free Masonry of friendly communication that animates all commercial travelers, to brothers on the road far and wide, and thousands of appreciative guests have crossed its hospitable threshold in the short year of its existence. It aims to fulfill in the highest degree the purpose of a social organization. It affords its Members the benefits of a perfectly ordered Club, free from the surroundings that so often make club life an objectionable thing. It offers to a certain class of men a form of entertainment that is very dear to them, and which no class can better appreciate.

In the New York Club the Commercial Traveler can pleasantly extend the hospitality of a home to his customers and friends, and perhaps repay in some degree the friendly consideration and attention which has so often greeted him while on the road. There are no rigid rules to narrow the purpose of the Commercial Travelers Club, no Chinese Wall of exclusion to girdle it. It is, in the broadest, the most liberal, the freest sense, a Commercial Club for Commercial men. The Membership has grown steadily; it couldn't help growing, in view of the advantages offered. In the first place, the Members belong to the sort of men one likes to meet. Some of them are travelers; others are energetic commercial men; others are newspaper men; nearly all of them

J. M. Proctor Knott

are young, and *all* are good fellows. Then, again, the Members of the Club enjoy privileges which are remarkable when it is considered that the initiation fee is only $10, and the annual dues, $20.

The list of Club Officers elected at the last election in December embraces the following names: BOARD OF GOVERNORS: Geo. W. Proctor Knott, *President;* John G. Hart, *Vice-President;* Charles E. Matthews, *Treasurer;* Denis Tucker, *Secretary;* John L. Shepherd, Arthur S. Wilbligg, H. P. Beach, Geo. W. Graves, E. C. Mathewson, Martin S. White, John H. Willis, E. C. Carroll, E. F. Cronin, S. L. McGonigal, *Governors.*

These gentlemen, hailing from the City of New York, believed that an association wisely planned would be an excellent thing for themselves and for the fraternity in general. They did better than merely discuss the matter. They boldly resolved to put the idea to a thorough test. A more extended personal mention of the founders and governors of the Club will follow, and be found with their portraits. The handsome Club House is located at No. 15 West 31st Street, and here the latch-string always hangs out and a cordial welcome awaits the wayfaring commercial man. The interest manifested in the Club, as shown in many ways and most recently by the patronage given this publication, we most highly appreciate, and sincerely hope that the future growth and prosperity of the organization may be such as to justify the kindness and confidence manifested toward it.

George W. Proctor Knott, ELECTED PRESIDENT AT ANNUAL MEETING, DECEMBER, 1891, AND AGAIN UNANIMOUSLY CHOSEN AT SECOND ANNUAL ELECTION, SEPTEMBER, 1892. (Portrait, opposite page.) Mr. Knott was born in Lebanon, Ky., July 10, 1856, and is of Irish-American parents, his father being of the celebrated family of that name for which Kentucky is famous, and his mother the seventh daughter of a Belfast clergyman of the Church of England. It is easy to see that from such stock a bright boy should be born, and the subject of this sketch is the result.

When a baby in arms his parents moved North and determined upon making New York their home —it is to this that George owes his education, as he was enabled to attend the public schools for which this city is noted, and to graduate from Grammar School No. 28, in West 40th Street, with honor. Entering the College of the City of New York, he took the commercial course, after which he secured a cadetship to West Point. The system of study and training at the Military School proved too hard; after six months' trial he was not strong enough to stand the strain of being a young soldier, so he resigned and returned home to New York.

His father then secured him a position with the Tower Manufacturing Company, the great stationers and importers of Broadway, and with them he rapidly advanced from the ranks to a road position, and became one of their most successful travelers. In 1885 he accepted a flattering offer tendered him by Mr. Geo. A. Raisbeck, the President of the Ph. Hake Manufacturing Company, located at 132 and 134 Essex Street, this city, and makers of fine cards and ladies' stationery, with a world-wide reputation, where he again demonstrated his ability to keep moving upward by being admitted into this famous firm as Secretary, January, 1894.

Mr. Knott is very fond of all kinds of sports, likes horses, is a crank on baseball, and is a good all-around athlete himself. While at college he used to run hurdle and flat races, and has done a hundred yards in ten and a quarter seconds, under the colors of the "Mercury foot." He is a

CHARLES E. MATTHEWS.

See page 1).

First President, Founder and Member Board of Governors, 1889.

Treasurer Commercial Travelers Club of New York, 1893

man of slight build and medium height, served his seven years in the gallant Seventh Regiment, and is a member of the Veteran organization and club, as well as of several others. His manners are pleasant and affable, he is a ready talker, a fair speechmaker, and a great leader and organizer. He is a firm disciplinarian, but kind-hearted and possessed of a keen sense of humor, is fair to all, has no favorites, treating all alike for the good and welfare of the Club.

His forte is his executive ability, and as a chairman and presiding officer he stands high, being well posted as a parliamentarian. He believes in making friends of every one. His brother travelers all like him, and his clubmates look to him as the fountain head and acknowledged leader of this great, glorious, and grand movement of Travelers Clubs. During the past winter he endeavored to do much in the way of securing members from the Commercial Travelers Brotherhood and other organizations as members of the Travelers Club, and with great success. His assiduity to business and the necessity of keeping on the road have kept him from giving more attention personally to the affairs of the Club.

Charles E. Matthews, ELECTED TREASURER, COMMERCIAL TRAVELERS CLUB, DECEMBER, 1892. (Portrait, see p. 12.) Mr. Matthews' name was on the card that called a meeting to consider the advisability of starting a Commercial Travelers Club. He was Chairman of that meeting, and was elected First President of the Commercial Travelers Club of New York City. In a hot contest for the Treasurership he was elected by an overwhelming majority. He is leading traveler for William Schwarzwaelder & Company, Office Furniture dealers in New York City, at No. 37 Fulton Street. During the early days of the Club Mr. Matthews spent much of his time in the clubhouse in the preliminary work of organization. He went through much drudgery for the sake of the Club, and his attention was fully appreciated by the boys. Later on he married an estimable lady and settled down at Port Richmond, Staten Island. Mr. Matthews is a typical traveler, and enjoys the confidence of his employer, Hon. William Schwarzwaelder, who is Trustee of the Club. The attachments and friendships of Mr. Matthews are strong and lasting. He is the bitter foe of all forms of usurpation and injustice; he does not stand on personal grounds in his official capacity, but deals out even-handed justice to all concerned. As Treasurer, the funds of the Club are in safe hands. As a business man he is conservative and careful in all his dealings. No better selection could have been made for the position he holds. Ever courteous and conciliatory, he graciously attends to his duties. Under his suggestion and management the Club has prospered, and before he surrenders the portfolio of the Treasurership, there is no doubt that the Club will be on a safe and substantial footing for the future. The boys all wish Charlie success and prosperity.

* *

Mr. John Gladys Hart, ELECTED VICE-PRESIDENT, COMMERCIAL TRAVELERS CLUB, AT THE ANNUAL ELECTION IN DECEMBER, 1892. (Portrait, see p. 14.) Mr. John Gladys Hart was born September 3, 1863, in Cork, Ireland, and left there at the age of six years, going to London, England. He was educated at Exeter College, from which he graduated when he was 15 years old. He then entered

LATEST PHOTOGRAPH BY FALK

John G. Hart

the employ of William Whiteley & Company. "The Universal Provider," Westbourne Grove, London, which he had to abandon on account of ill health. After traveling all over Europe in search of health, he was advised to go to the United States, which he did, arriving here March 1st, 1880. His first location was at Bismarck, North Dakota. Subsequently he entered the employ of Seltz, Schwab & Co., Chicago, and remained with them about two years, after which he went to Boston to engage with Batchelder & Lincoln, for whom he worked about six years. He then engaged with Rice & Hutchins, of Boston, his present employers, in connection with their New York Agency, the Manhattan Shoe Company. Mr. Hart was one of the first to see the need of a Club for New York traveling men, and, with two others, organized the present Club. Mr. Hart is a traveler whom any one would be glad to meet on the road; he is hail-fellow-well-met, and has wonderful ability in securing and maintaining a personal popularity with other men. He recently married a noble lady, and has settled down for life. It was during Mr. Hart's administration that the Club was incorporated and the present Club House fitted up and opened.

Arthur Shirley Willdigg, MEMBER OF BOARD OF GOVERNORS AND CHAIRMAN OF COMMITTEE ON NEW CLUB HOUSE, COMMERCIAL TRAVELERS CLUB OF NEW YORK. (Portrait, see p. 16.) Mr. Arthur S. Willdigg was born in Birmingham, England, September 22, 1859. He came to this country with his parents in 1870, and attended Grammar School No. 34, New York City. He afterward learned the trade of machinist, that being his father's business. He devoted five years to learning this trade, and had many inducements offered him to remain in the machine business; but he did not like it, gave it up, and took Horace Greeley's advice, and went West. He then started to sell goods for Martin Kalbfleisch's Sons, the Bushwick Chemical Works, and was with them from the day he took his maiden trip until they failed in business some few years ago. After their failure, he started in for the Cleveland Baking Powder Company, for which he sold goods in nearly every city in the Union. He has been on the road upward of twelve years. Mr. Willdigg is married, and has two sons. He lives in the City of Brooklyn, N. Y. He is now stationed in New York City for the Cleveland Baking Powder Co., selling to the grocery trade. Mr. Willdigg has traits that make him a foremost traveler. In searching for the picture of a typical American traveler, the artist picked out the photograph of Mr. Willdigg, and his picture adorns the cover of this work. It was fortunate for the Commercial Travelers of New York that Mr. Willdigg was in a position to devote much of his time to the building up of the organization. As Chairman of the Committee in charge of the work of securing all the substantial results, he has distinguished himself by success, and had he been allowed the freedom which his ability entitled him to, even greater results would have been attained. His honesty and sincerity burn with a steady flame; he knows no turning from the right. He is the soul of honor. To those who know him intimately, his friendship is highly prized. Once your friend, he knows no swerving from the path of loyalty. It is owing to this sterling trait of his character that he wins so many fast and loyal friends. With one beck of his finger, he can call around him more staunch supporters and allies than any other young man of his age in Brooklyn. The highest tribute that can be paid him is that he is faithful. It is the highest recommendation that any man can have among his fellow-men. Mr. Willdigg's executive ability is remarkable, and will some day place him in the front rank of the enterprising commercial men of this country.

ARTHUR S WILLDIGG

Pres.dent and Member   of
      Committee   New Che ie   3
        Te   N

George W. Graves, CHAIRMAN COMMITTEE ON MEMBERSHIP, COMMERCIAL TRAVELERS CLUB. (Portrait, see p. 18.) Mr. Graves has a larger personal acquaintance with the retail stove trade, and Commercial Travelers in general, than any other one person. Don't take it for granted that the middle letter of his name stands for Washington, as you might make the mistake of your life some day by addressing the subject of our sketch as George Washington Graves. People have been killed for committing what Graves would consider a less offense than that.

George William Graves was born in the city of Rochester, N. Y., in 1848, and finished his education at the Rochester Academy. He started early in life in the stove business as a traveler for S. H. Ransom & Co., of Albany, who at that time were one of the largest stove manufacturers in the world. He remained with that firm nine years, during which time he made several novel inventions in stove construction which are considered very valuable patents.

In 1885 he accepted the position of Eastern Manager at Buffalo for the Peninsular Stove Co., of Detroit, Mich., and held the management until 1888, when he resigned, to become interested in the manufacture of Manhattan Stoves with Eugene Munsell & Co., 218 Water Street, of this city, where he still remains, besides being a member of the firm of Beaton & Graves, New Britain, Conn.

During his residence in Buffalo, he was the head and front of any and all organizations that tended to advance the interests of Commercial Travelers. For three years he was the President of Post C. T. P. A., and it was the most successful organization of its kind in the State. He was one of the incorporators, and the first President, of the Travelers Club of Buffalo, whose peculiar and successful features have been copied by other Clubs throughout the country. He is one of the incorporators of this Club, and is now serving as State President of the Travelers' Protective Accidental Insurance Co. Mr. Graves has few equals and no superior as a presiding officer. He recognizes no cliques, personalities, nor coteries. In this regard he is like James G. Blaine, the great statesman and politician, who won the esteem of Democrats as well as Republicans by absolute fairness in all his rulings when speaker of the House.

Kind to his friends, and considerate to all, we are glad to illustrate this work with the portrait of one who has always been interested in the welfare of Commercial Travelers, and has done more than duty required.

* *

Mr. John L. Shepherd, MEMBER OF BOARD OF GOVERNORS, COMMERCIAL TRAVELERS CLUB OF NEW YORK. (Portrait, see p. 20.) Mr. John L. Shepherd is also President of the New England Traveling Jewelers' Association of Boston, and Vice-President of the Long Island Wheelmen of Brooklyn, N. Y.; also a member of a number of prominent social clubs in New York and Brooklyn, in all of which he takes a prominent part. For a number of years Mr. Shepherd was engaged in the newspaper business, and for some time published a Sunday morning paper in St. Louis, Mo. He is a native of Virginia, and Agent of the Keystone Watch Case Company, the largest concern of this kind in the world, its product running as high as twenty-five hundred cases a day, in the best season. His office is at No. 23 Maiden Lane, and is the finest furnished office in the trade. Mr. Shepherd can always be found there, and all Commercial Travelers will ever receive a hearty welcome. Mr. Shepherd is a brilliant orator, and renowned as the Story Teller of the Club. He is known as "Genial John"; a man who has been President of

GEORGE W. GRAVES

See page 17

Chairman Board of Governors, 1933

Commercial Travelers Club of New York

the American Jewelers' Association, and one withal whom it is well to know. He has made his mark in the jewelry trade as Manager of the Keystone Watch Case Company, and is universally beloved and admired by his fellows. He has added much to the conservative element of The Commercial Travelers and wisdom to its councils.

***

Mr. John H. Willis, CHAIRMAN OF THE HOUSE COMMITTEE, COMMERCIAL TRAVELERS CLUB OF NEW YORK. (Portrait, see p. 22.) Mr. John H. Willis was born in New York City in 1859, but in his early youth his parents removed to Massachusetts, and he received his education in the schools of that State. After a life divided between school and work on a farm, which continued until he was seventeen years of age, Mr. Willis entered upon a commercial career by connecting himself with a house engaged in the music trade, in Lowell, Mass., where he remained for eight years. He has a host of friends in the town which boasts of being the cradle of his business life, but his active and energetic mind became restless under the limits of such a circumscribed field. After leaving Lowell he spent two years in experimenting with the planting and development of an orange grove in Florida, and then came to New York, where he has since succeeded in building up a very lucrative business in the grocery trade. At the same time he has given considerable attention to real estate operations, in which he has been eminently successful. Six years ago he married a most estimable lady, and they boast to-day of a family of two children. Mr. Willis is known as "Honest John." With such a cognomen, it would be superfluous to add anything as to his honesty and integrity of purpose. Under his management as Chairman of the House Committee of the Commercial Travelers Club of New York, a very superior system of organization has been developed, the natural result of which is that the affairs of the Club are now running more smoothly than in the past.

***

Martin S. White, FOUNDER AND MEMBER OF BOARD OF GOVERNORS, AND MEMBER OF COMMITTEE ON NEW CLUB HOUSE, COMMERCIAL TRAVELERS CLUB OF NEW YORK. (Portrait, see p. 24.) Mr. Martin S. White was born Dec. 24, 1865. He was the youngest in a family of four children. When nine months old, his father died. His mother, a high-minded, intellectual, noble woman, gave him a good education, and he left college at the age of sixteen to enter upon a business career with a commission house. He proved very industrious, and developed good business qualities. When not quite eighteen years of age, he was sent on the road, and proved a successful salesman from the start, making friends everywhere. He is well known to the fancy goods and novelty trade, and is a familiar figure through the South and West. Owing to his invincible activity and energy, some of his friends call him "The Irrepressible White." If there is one trait to be admired more than another about Mr. White, it is his integrity of purpose; he is a stickler for commercial honor, and is always making a stern fight for Right and Truth. Whenever there is a "scrap," White will be found on the side of the right, and in behalf of justice. Mr. White was one of the founders of the Club, and gave more of his time and energy to its interests than any other member, except Mr. Willdigg, in the start out, and during the dark days of the Commercial Travelers Club, when those who now are prominent were mere on-lookers. He has been twice elected to the Board of Governors, and is the most popular member belonging to the New York

JOHN L. SHEPHERD.

See page 17.

Member Board of Governors, 1892-'3

Raconteur and After-dinner Orator,
Commercial Travelers Club of New York

21

Club. If Martin will work on some commercial deal with the same zeal with which he labors for the Club's interests, he will be on top of the heap in the business world.

* *

Homer P. Beach, ELECTED MEMBER OF THE BOARD OF GOVERNORS OF THE COMMERCIAL TRAVELERS CLUB OF NEW YORK, 1892 AND 1893. (Portrait, see page 26.) Mr. Homer P. Beach is a well-known citizen, not only in New York but in the country generally. As an organizer he has few equals and no superiors. This was shown in the caucuses preceding the annual election of officers of the Commercial Travelers Club, of which he is one of the most popular members. His well-known zeal and activity in connection with anything he undertakes, insure great advantages to any organization securing him as a member or an officer. Mr. Beach is very popular in the district where he resides and quite influential in political circles, and a candidate who secures his support is quite sure to be elected with a large majority. His connection with the Eagle Pencil Co. has been many years, and he has done more to create demand for lead pencils of American make and encourage this industry in the United States than any other man. He is not only a very popular traveler but a successful business man, and in his special line he is much sought for to aid in the promotion of other enterprises in which he does not take an active, so much as a directing, interest. His judgment is always good in matters of administration or finesse. Among the characteristics of Mr. Beach is his retiring, unassuming modesty, but those who enjoy his friendship know how loyal and faithful he is. Mr. Beach is a member of the brotherhood of the Commercial Travelers Club and numerous other Associations, and on the whole is voted as being a good, genial, wholesouled fellow.

*

Mr. S. L. McGonigal, CHAIRMAN ENTERTAINMENT COMMITTEE, COMMERCIAL TRAVELERS CLUB OF NEW YORK. (Portrait, page 28.) Mr. McGonigal was born in Dover, Delaware, July 19, 1861. He went to the public school, and also to Wilmington Conference Academy, in his native town. He left home when seventeen years of age and went to Philadelphia, engaging in the gentlemen's furnishing goods business. He remained there five years, and then went to North Carolina and began business in the general mercantile line on his own account. His life while there was a very quiet one, on account of there being only about two hundred people in the village; no post-office nearer than twelve miles, and no railroad nearer than thirty miles. It might be added here that the store was run in connection with the saw-mill business; hence the reason for being so far away from any large town. After he was there a while he succeeded in establishing a post-office with a daily mail, and was made first postmaster. He remained there until all the near-by timber was cut up, and then sold out his interest, moving to New York City, where he started as a shirt manufacturer and dealer in men's furnishing goods. This business he has pursued with wonderful success, his genial qualities and business tact being used to build up a large trade. He is one of the organizers of the Commercial Travelers Club, and has been on the Board of Governors for two terms, and as Chairman of the Entertainment Committee he has done much to build up the social side of the organization. At the "Smokers" given from time to

JO-N H. WILL S.

time, his genius for the position he holds is brilliantly shown. He always secures the best of dramatic talent at these entertainments, and his management of the "Smokers" is the pleasure of the boys.

*

Edward Clayton Mathewson, MEMBER OF THE BOARD OF GOVERNORS, COMMERCIAL TRAVELERS CLUB. (Portrait, see p. 30.) Mr. Edward Clayton Mathewson was born in Lisle, New York State, March 24, 1867. It was originally intended that he should take up the scholastic profession. In view of this he graduated from the Lisle Academy at the age of sixteen, and was at that time granted a certificate to teach in any part of the State. Although he graduated, his inclinations were not for a scholastic life, and he felt a mercantile career was more suited to his capabilities. He started out as a produce merchant on his own account, in Greenwich Street, New York City, where he continued for two years, and left at the end of that time, having been offered a position as traveler for a manufacturer of silver plate. Since then he has been with the following firms: manager of the American Machine Company for the New England States; salesman one year and manager two years for the Patent Cereals Company, 39 Pearl Street, New York City, and the same for Messrs. Alfred Bird & Sons, of Birmingham, England, being salesman, and now holding the position of manager of their Sales Department, for the United States. His relations with all these firms have been of the pleasantest kind, and he holds valuable testimonials from them. Mr. Mathewson is a distinguished traveler, and would be picked out from a crowd as a man of great force of character, and worthy of personal respect and attention. He was one of the organizers of this Club, being elected upon the first Board of Governors, and also unanimously elected for the present year.

If there is one thing more than another that characterizes his action, it is his judicial capacity, as he always acts in a conservative spirit, seeking the substantial results that follow good judgment.

On the road he is popular, and is held in high esteem by all who know him.

*

Ernest C. Carroll, FOUNDER, AND MEMBER OF THE BOARD OF GOVERNORS, COMMERCIAL TRAVELERS CLUB OF NEW YORK. (Portrait, see p. 32.) Mr. Ernest C. Carroll was born in the City of London, England, in 1865. He was educated at St. John's School, then under the direction of the Rev. W. T. T. Webber, who is now the Bishop of Brisbane. He also passed several terms at the North London Institute of Music, under the personal tuition of Mr. Louis Cottell. At an early age he entered the office of Adam Hill & Company, No. 258 High Holborn, London, one of the oldest firms of distillers in England, and remained with them for ten years. His first position in this country was as Secretary of the old Manhattan Cloak & Suit Co., in Broadway, which position he resigned to become the Western representative of Jacob Herman, 324 Canal St., New York, in whose interests he has for the past four years regularly traveled between Chicago and the Rocky Mountains, and has established a most enviable reputation. In London, Mr. Carroll was a well-known member of the Metropolitan, Churchill, and Supper Clubs, as well as being for several years a member of the famous Kildare B. & T. Club. The first impression of Mr. Carroll is that he is a finished gentleman. That he is a well-educated man, is evident on making his acquaintance. He was one of the founders of the Commercial Travelers

MARTIN S. WHITE,

Founder and Member Board of Governors of the
Commercial Travelers Club of New York

Club, and has given much of his time and attention in the furtherance of its interests. For a time he acted as Treasurer, and in every position he has held he has been above reproach. At the Annual Banquet of the Commercial Travelers Club, held in December in the banqueting hall of the Club-house, he made one of the finest orations of the evening. He possesses a sunny disposition, and is an amateur singer of much promise.

* *

Mr. E. F. Cronin, MEMBER OF THE BOARD OF GOVERNORS, COMMERCIAL TRAVELERS CLUB OF NEW YORK. (Portrait, see p. 34.) Mr. E. F. Cronin was formerly connected with the New York branch of the well-known packing house of Swift & Co., of Chicago. He left that establishment, however, two or three years ago to connect himself with Messrs. J. P. Scott & Co., one of the leading firms of wholesale jewelers in Maiden Lane, this city, where he still remains. He is highly esteemed by his employers for his faithfulness, integrity, and devotion to their best interests. Whatever he undertakes to do is done with his might, a disposition that has been conspicuous in the earnest and indefatigable services which he has rendered for the Commercial Travelers Club. Indeed, among the ardent and untiring workers having in mind the ultimate and permanent success of the Club, Mr. Cronin occupies a position in the front ranks. At the same time, he is extremely modest, and is always disposed to regard his own efforts in a subdued light.

*

Mr. Denis Tucker, ELECTED SECRETARY, COMMERCIAL TRAVELERS CLUB, AT THE ANNUAL ELECTION IN DECEMBER, 1892. (Portrait, see p. 36.) Mr. Denis Tucker was born in New York City, August 15, 1852, and educated in Public Schools Nos. 44 and 38, New York City; also No. 1, Stapleton, S. I. He began business life with the firm of T. C. Richards & Co., 47 Murray Street, New York City, with whom he remained five years. He then engaged with Speyer Bros., No. 110 Bowery, with whom he remained eight years. He has been ten years with the Taylor Company, 163 Bowery, this city. He is a member of the United Council No. 1035, A. L. of H.; also a member of Court P. W. Hart, No. 7670, A. O. F. of A.; also Tammany Association, 10th Assembly District; also Casket Salesman Protective Association; also Manhattan Council No. 12, Legion of Justice; also Manetuck Tribe No. 162, Imp. O. of R. M. Mr. Tucker is a gentleman of the highest integrity, worthy of any position to which he may be elected by his associates. He is careful and judicious in the office of Secretary of the Club, and especially wise in his prevention of those little unpleasantnesses that so often mar club life. If he ever grows weary in well-doing, he never shows it by word or look. The boys have much for which to thank him in return for his courteous bearing at all times, and above all, for his genial humor.

H. P. BEACH.

Member Board of Governors, 1 __ __
Commuter Travelers __ __ of New York.

THE PROBLEM OF TO-DAY.

AN ADDRESS TO THE LONG CAVALCADE OF COMMERCIAL TRAVELERS.

HE hour has come to organize. The Problem of To-day is to stop unnecessary competition, equalize commercial advantages, and prevent arbitrary discrimination. Asked how it is to be solved, the reply will be, with triple emphasis, *organization!* ORGANI-ZATION! ORGANIZATION! It is not fair that one-half the country should be organized and not the other half. While nondescript orators out of a political job, and reformers with a large mortgage on Utopia, are advancing visionary schemes to fit other times and conditions more or less remote, cut-throat competition goes on, which leads to destructive results and inflicts a monstrous wrong upon the commerce of our country.

The fact of the matter is, we must inaugurate the greatest fight in this country by any class of men to stop unnecessary competition. Every morning two hundred thousand travelers go forth in the struggle to secure orders and, if possible, maintain living prices, so that we may be able to pay first-class railroad fares and hotel rates. Individually we are unable to maintain prices in the fight, but collectively we can do it. Incompetent men who depend entirely upon breaking prices to maintain or secure trade have been driven from the road, while those who remain are travelers who hold their trade by their personal influence and ability to show the quality and grade of their goods, instead of depending upon a broken price to hold their own.

Now, you ask how this is to be done. It is a difficult matter to put the answer on paper, but we will attempt to simplify it. We will take an illustration: Suppose that a manufacturer, who sells his goods over the entire country, desires to place a new engine or boiler plant in his manufactory, and asks for bids of the boiler makers and engine builders. Now, under strict organization, the travelers' committee, representing that branch of manufacture, have made a limit to the prices, below which no traveler can go and pay first-class rates of fare along with other expenses. All of the engine builders keep within the stipulated limit except one, who makes a discount or break from the stipulated price. The traveler on the committee of the boiler trade reports to the general committee, and the general committee sends a representative to the purchaser, and we say to him: "We are spending our time and money to maintain prices; now, if you take that engine plant, it will be at the peril of your trade; you will antagonize in so doing the two hundred thousand travelers who are interested in the maintenance of this price, and who control the trade of this continent." In just such a case as this, in every instance, will the battle be won.

All the heavy distributing and supply houses are necessarily with us in the fight to stop the

S. L. McGONIGAL.

Bricklayer

Member Board of Governors, 1902-3.

Chairman Entertainment Committee

Chairman Finance Cttee. 1903.

cut-throat policy, and the favors of heavy freighters will be thrown where the travelers desire. We now furnish three-fourths of the freight shipments in less than car-load lots, and control one-third of the passenger traffic of the entire country. We pay one million dollars every day to railroads and hotels, while the total annual disbursements to maintain the system are upwards of one thousand millions of dollars. It behooves us to be reasonable and use our concentrated power wisely, for already we see the Farmers' Alliance, to which all eyes were turned with burning hope for the future, used as an engine of destruction in the futile attempt to lock up the products of the soil. Agitate. Speak to your brother knights of the grip. Tell them the time is ripe for action. Moving as a solid phalanx, will be added to the highest activity, greater social power, the result of organization. For has it not been written: "Seest thou a man diligent in his business; he shall stand before kings; he shall not stand before mean men."

Now, Brother Members, remain true to your Club, if you are members of a Club. If you are not, then join the Club in the locality from which you hail. This membership will give you the entrée to all other Travelers Clubs throughout the country under the auspices of the National League of Clubs. There are advantages to be gained from organization; advantages to yourselves, advantages to your fellow citizens, and advantages to the business of the whole country. Organize; organize to protect your interests, organize to protect the interests of Brother Travelers in all parts of the country. Any disadvantage that may occur to you, any wrongs that may be inflicted upon you, any injustice that may be practiced upon you, will be the result of your own negligence to protect your own interests. Protect those interests, protect yourselves, and every organization, social and political, throughout the country, will respect us. Organization is necessary to protect our interests as travelers; to secure that common respect requisite to a proper conception of those rights which are our due. Organize upon the club idea and maintain that organization, pay dues to your Club, attend the meetings of your Club regularly, and the time will not be far distant when you will see the practical results of organized effort, and devotion to your Club. In that hope, accept the kindest wishes of all earnest workers for the success of the National League of Travelers Clubs.—R. R. F.

E. C. MATHEWSON.

NEW YORK CAPITAL.

THE financial strength of New York's fiduciary institutions is shown by the vast accumulations in the National Banks, Trust Companies, Savings Banks, and numerous other corporations controlling the wealth centered here. Of course, the commercial supremacy of New York is undoubted. This port has the lion's share of the trade of the country. The following is a fair statement of the financial power of the metropolis:

Deposits of New York City Banks, (Largely secured by Railroad Stocks and Bonds.)	Half a Thousand Million Dollars.
Assets of Life Insurance Companies,	Half a Thousand Million Dollars.
Resources of Savings Banks, -	Four Hundred Million Dollars.
Strength of Trust Companies,	Three Hundred Million Dollars.
Aggregate of smaller Institutions,	Three Hundred Million Dollars.
GRAND TOTAL, -	Two Thousand Million Dollars.

THE TWO HUNDRED THOUSAND TRAVELERS OF THIS COUNTRY CONTROL THE TRADE OF THE CONTINENT.

Representatives of New York Capital, - (Salesmen from our great Commercial Houses.)	One Hundred Thousand Travelers.
From other Distributing Centers, -	One Hundred Thousand Travelers.
They pay to Railroads and Hotels,	- One Million Dollars Per Day.
Book three-fourths of the entire Freight, (In less than car load lots.)	800 Million Tons Per Year.

E. C. CARROLL.

Founder and Member Board of Governors, 18 2-93,
Commercial Travelers Club of New York.

A GLIMPSE OF "THE STREET."

IT is not so very long ago that our fathers built a wall of brush and trees on the lower part of Manhattan Island to keep the wolves and bears from the little fold of fortune-hunters that had gathered on the bay, and to prevent the sheep and cows from straying into the forest during the day. That was the beginning of Wall Street—of what is now even a much stronger bulwark that has been erected to protect the interests, not of Manhattan Island alone, but of the whole country. It is to-day the financial center of the United States, and the time is rapidly approaching when it will unquestionably occupy an equally important position as regards the whole civilized world. Shrewd financiers, both in this country and Europe, admit that the time is not so very far distant when New York will control (as London does to-day) the commercial and financial operations of every nation on the globe.

The Foreign Commerce of the United States now approximates two thousand million dollars yearly, in value. In the last fiscal year we sent abroad, of the products of the forests, the mines, and the soil, more than a thousand million dollars' worth of goods, which we had no other use for. These figures represent the surplus, the overflow of a country which, less than a century ago, had fewer inhabitants than can be found within the limits of the State of New York to-day. One-half the railroads of the world are within our borders. Fifty per cent. of the total imports of wheat into the United Kingdom are obtained from "the States," and there is no other country in the world whose annual product of that cereal equals ours. We are clothing the world with cotton goods, or, at least, we are supplying the material from which they are produced, and the cotton crop of the Southern States has grown to be so large that no doubt is left but that, if railroad or other transportation facilities should be sufficiently improved, we may be equally able to supply the demands of Mars and a few other outlying planets.

In such wonderful strides as this country has made during the past fifty years in the development of its industries and in the establishment of a position which to-day is second to none among the great nations of the world, a combination of interests was an absolute necessity; indeed, we see the imperative necessity of combination in almost every enterprise of importance in which the people are engaged. Ten thousand millions of dollars, which were necessary to build and equip the railroads of the country, could have been obtained in no other way. The bank capital required to conduct the business could be found only by a union of investors and capitalists. This aggregation of capital and unity of interests among people engaged in like pursuits has become an *absolute necessity* also, on account of the greater economy, as well as the more perfect and quicker results that can thus

E   LE NIN.

Vom.

N Y S.

be secured. It was only natural that the extension of such a policy should meet with opposition. The weaklings—those who by improvidence or for other reasons were unable to coöperate—inevitably became enemies, and the demagogues in both Political and Social organizations quickly detected a convenient club of large size with which to belabor capital on one side, and hoodwink their dupes on the other. Still, the good work has gone on. As the result, what do we see?

The new securities listed on the New York Stock Exchange during the past year aggregated nearly $300,000,000. The transactions in railroad and other stocks footed up nearly 86,000,000 shares, having a par value of about $8,000,000,000. Purchases and sales of railroad and other bonds exceeded $500,000,000 more. It is a most remarkable fact that all these securities were bought and sold on the good faith, the honor, that exists between the members of the Stock Exchange. A little pencil memorandum made at the time of the transactions furnished the only evidence for the time being that the stock or bond had been bought or sold; yet, there was not a single lawsuit between the members on account of differences that may have arisen regarding these operations. In fact, lawsuits are not admitted among members of the Exchange. If a misunderstanding is discovered at once, it is often settled by the toss of a penny, and "heads" or "tails" determines the issue; otherwise, an appeal to the proper committee is all that is necessary. That committee's decision is final. In the settlements from day to day of such monumental transactions, it is needless to say that an enormous amount of money is required. But the money of the Wall Street Banks is not all used in carrying on Stock Exchange operations; on the contrary, more than one-half the foreign trade of the whole country passes through the Port of New York. And this is not all. At the time of the moving of the crops from either the West or the South, New York Banks are called upon to supply millions upon millions of money to assist in the handling of the merchandise—in paying the farmer for his product, and carrying the goods until they are finally disposed of.

It will not seem especially surprising, therefore, that the deposits of the New York Banks range from $450,000,000 to $550,000,000, throughout the year—an enormous sum to be constantly on hand, subject to check or withdrawal. As compared with other cities, it is interesting to note that the checks which pass through the New York Clearing House from year to year amount to nearly 60 per cent. of all the clearances of all the cities from Maine to California. In 1892 the New York clearings aggregated almost $37,000,000,000. While there are sixty-one banks belonging to the New York Clearing House Association, the bulk of the enormous business referred to is transacted by a few down-town banks. Among the most prominent of these are the Park, which carries the heaviest line of deposits of any bank in the United States, and which is presided over by Mr. E. K. Wright; the First National, at the corner of Wall Street and Broadway, which does a larger business with other banks scattered in all parts of the country than any of its associates, and which is also always directly concerned in some of the leading railroad enterprises of the day; and the Chase National, which owes its wonderful success in recent years chiefly to the great financial ability and popularity of its president, Mr. H. W. Cannon.

DEN S TUCKER.

New York 1893

STATEMENT OF THE ASSOCIATED BANKS OF THE CITY OF NEW YORK.

FROM REPORTS TO THE NEW YORK CLEARING HOUSE, AS REQUIRED UNDER SECTION 16 OF THE CONSTITUTION, FOR WEEK ENDING SATURDAY, MARCH 11, 1893.

Nos.	BANKS.	CAPITAL	SURPLUS	LOANS.	SPECIE.	LEGALS	DEPOSITS	CIRCULATION	Nos.
1	Bank of N. Y. National Banking Assoc'n	$2,000,000	$2,998,500						1
2	Manhattan Company								2
3	Merchants' National								3
4	Mechanics' National								4
5	Bank of America								5
6	Phenix National								6
7	National City								7
8	Tradesmen's National								8
9	Chemical National								9
10	Merchants' Exchange National								10
11	Gallatin National								11
12	National Butchers' and Drovers'								12
13	Mechanics' and Traders'								13
14	Greenwich								14
15	Leather Manufacturers' National								15
16	Seventh National								16
17	Bank of the State of New York								17
18	American Exchange National								18
19	National Bank of Commerce								19
20	National Broadway								20
21	Mercantile National								21
22	Pacific								22
23	National Bank of the Republic								23
24	Chatham National								24
25	People's								25
26	National Bank of North America								26
27	Hanover National								27
28	Irving National								28
29	National Citizens'								29
30	Nassau Bank								30
31	Market and Fulton National								31
32	St. Nicholas Bank of New York								32
33	National Shoe and Leather								33
34	Corn Exchange								34
35	Continental National								35
36	Oriental								36
37	Importers' and Traders' National								37
38	National Park								38
39	East River National								39
40	Fourth "								40
41	Central "								41
42	Second "								42
43	Ninth "								43
44	First "								44
45	Third "								45
46	New York National Exchange								46
47	Bowery Bank								47
48	New York County National								48
49	German-American								49
50	Chase National								50
51	Fifth Avenue								51
52	German Exchange								52
53	Germania								53
54	United States National								54
55	Lincoln National								55
56	Garfield "								56
57	Fifth "								57
58	Bank of the Metropolis								58
59	West Side								59
60	Seaboard National								60
61	Sixth "								61
62	Western "								62
63	First National Bank, Brooklyn								63
64	Southern National								64

	TOTAL, NATIONAL BANKS	$	$					
	STATE BANKS							
	Totals							

Reserve, $1,800,050. Decrease

* As per official reports. 46 National Banks, Dec. 9, 1892. 18 State Banks, Dec. 15, 1892.

Clearings for week ending March 11, 1893.		
" March 1, 1893.		
Balances " March 11, 1893.		
" March 4, 1893.		
Clearings this day March 11, 1893.		
Balances " March 11, 1893.		

PHOTOGRAPHED BY FALK

THOMAS C. PLATT.

EN who know Thomas C. Platt love him. Men who don't know him, estimate his character and his usefulness according to the glass through which they look. For twenty-five years he has been prominent before the nation as a politician, a member of Congress, a statesman, a United States Senator, a party manager, a man of large commercial interests, and an influential social factor. It would be odd if, while pushing along these various avenues with vigor, energy, pluck, and well-outlined plan of procedure, he failed to jostle, to come in conflict with, to injure the plans and programmes of other people. That Mr. Platt ever intentionally injured mortal man, no one who knows him believes, unless it were in a fair eye to eye fight, where the chances were equal, and hitting below the belt an impossibility. He is a many-sided individuality.

It would be difficult for one who had never seen him away from home, unless indeed it were when, having forsaken the beastly torridities of the metropolis, he found rest and comfort, solace and refreshment, on the broad piazzas of the Oriental at Manhattan Beach, to imagine him other than a mild-mannered, courteous, sweet-tempered gentleman of retiring disposition, preferring isolation to companionship. But he is no such man.

We, who are familiar with the bitter contests waged on the political field, know that courage is as essential as diplomacy, that stubbornness, even a grade beyond the line of firmness, is at times an absolute essential. Mr. Platt is regarded everywhere as a conscientious man. Having once made up his mind that a specified course is the best for his party, he adheres to it with tenacity, and nothing could compel him to change his programme. Loyalty has ever been a conspicuous feature in his composition, as was clearly shown by his masterful leadership in Chicago, where the famous three hundred and six stood together while the ship went down. No face is more familiar than his to the readers of political and comic literature. He has been over-praised by friends and unfairly censured by hostile critics, but I have never seen or heard of a charge that he was unfaithful to trust, disloyal to conviction, or party to any measure which suggested peril to the Republic or defeat to his organization. Personally, Mr. Platt is a charm.

It used to be said that the man who wrote, "You can catch more flies with molasses than vinegar," had Mr. Platt in mind when he formulated that bit of wisdom. However that may be, there is no doubt that if he were a European, rather than an American, and had circumstances favored his adoption of a diplomatic career, he would have proved a monumental success. In personal intercourse, all who meet him recognize the amiability of his nature, the considerateness of his conduct, the delight of his conversation, not failing to carry with them, however, a conviction of the sturdy independence of his character, and the all around excellence of his views concerning men and measures. Although an intense Republican in politics, he is first and above all else an American, believing firmly in the principles announced in the Declaration of Independence and the Constitution of the United States, the necessity of our common schools, and the desirability of the loyalty of fanaticism even, to the emblem of the Republic, Old Glory, the Stars and Stripes.

COMMERCIAL SUPREMACY OF NEW YORK.

THE aggregate value of the foreign commerce of the Port of New York during the fiscal year ending June 30th, 1892, amounted to $1,061,220,878, which is more than one-half the total of the United States, which was $2,010,311,036.

The chief imports, as regards value, were:

Sugar and molasses, for Port of New York	$18,354,286
Sugar and molasses, for all other U. S. Ports	58,932,271
Coffee, for Port of New York	112,662,499
Coffee, for all other U. S. Ports	15,379,131
Tea, for Port of New York	10,081,372
Tea, for all other U. S. Ports	1,291,850
Manufactures of wood, for Port of New York	29,791,209
Manufactures of wood, for all other U. S. Ports	5,771,670
Manufactures of silk, for Port of New York	27,761,396
Manufactures of silk, for all other U. S. Ports	3,441,688
Manufactures of cotton, for Port of New York	21,337,770
Manufactures of cotton, for all other U. S. Ports	6,986,071
Manufactures of flax, for Port of New York	18,043,684
Manufactures of flax, for all other U. S. Ports	8,249,533
Manufactures of hides and skins, other than furs, for Port of New York,	$18,715,491
Manufactures of hides and skins, other than furs, for all other U. S. Ports	8,134,727
Manufactures of tin, for Port of New York	12,978,800
Manufactures of tin, for all other U. S. Ports	8,004,632
Manufactures of india-rubber and gutta-percha, for Port of New York	18,533,343
Manufactures of india-rubber and gutta-percha, for all other U. S. Ports	1,299,747
Manufactures of tobacco, for Port of New York	8,932,949
Manufactures of tobacco, for all other U. S. Ports	4,495,668
Manufactures of precious stones, for Port of New York	11,288,275
Manufactures of precious stones, for all other U. S. Ports	1,066,145
Manufactures of raw silks, for Port of New York	8,925,938
Manufactures of raw silks, for all other U. S. Ports	15,395,556
Manufactures of wool, for Port of New York	6,831,821
Manufactures of wool, for all other U. S. Ports	13,356,287

Manufactures of wines, for Port of
New York $6,842,574
Manufactures of wines, for all other
U. S. Ports.............   2,101,929

The total value of the foreign imports during the year, for the United
States, was $897,057,002, of which
there was imported through New
York   576,246,119

Among the chief articles of export were:

Cotton, from Port of New York.... $34,773,589
Cotton, from all other U. S. Ports...   223,687,852
Breadstuffs, from Port of New York.   112,553,155
Breadstuffs, from all other U. S.
Ports........   187,809,662
Provisions, from Port of New York..   81,531,963
Provisions, from all other U. S.
Ports....   58,830,196
Mineral oils, from Port of New York.   32,896,657

Mineral oils, from all other U. S.
Ports........................ $16,891,620
Tobacco, from Port of New York...   14,719,978
Tobacco, from all other U. S. Ports.,   10,019,447
Cotton goods, from Port of New York,   10,638,601
Cotton goods, from all other U. S.
Ports   2,587,676
Cattle, from Port of New York..   14,227,753
Cattle, from all other U. S. Ports   20,871,342

The total value of our domestic exports for the year, for the entire
country, was $1,075,818,429, of which
New York's share was..   461,792,231

The total foreign commerce of New York was
$61,329,243 in excess of the preceding year, and
the excess for the entire country was $135,730,941.
The excess of imports over exports at this port was
$114,473,888, and for the entire United States the
excess was $178,761,427.

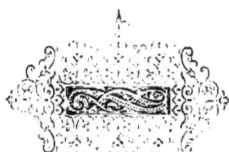

THOMAS POWELL FOWLER,

PRESIDENT OF THE NEW YORK, ONTARIO AND WESTERN RAILWAY COMPANY.

MONG the many Newburgh men who have come prominently before the public and who have attained high honor and distinction for sterling qualities and native talents, few are better known or more generally respected in railroad circles, or have been more successful in the legal profession, than the subject of this brief sketch. He was born in Newburgh, October 26, 1851. His father, Isaac Sebring Fowler, was a descendant of Isaac Fowler, who settled near this city in 1717. His mother, Mary Ludlow Powell, was the daughter of Robert Ludlow Powell, who was the son of Thomas Powell, long prominent in the affairs of the Empire State, and one of the most successful men of his time. His great-grandmother, Mary Powell, was in every way a remarkable woman; she was possessed of great talent and judgment, which were much appreciated in society. Her name is inseparably linked with the steam navigation of the Hudson River, and is familiar as a household word with the oldest as well as the youngest traveler on American steamboats. Mr. Fowler's childhood was spent at Newburgh. He received his early education at Siglar's School, Newburgh, and College Hill, Poughkeepsie, after which he studied abroad for nearly two years, spending most of his time in Germany. Returning to New York, he entered the banking house of Morton, Bliss & Co., then Morton, Burns & Co. where he acquired a general knowledge of financial affairs. We next find him studying law under Prof. Theo. D. Dwight, at the Columbia College Law School. He entered the junior class of that institution October 21, 1872. He pursued a full course of study, graduating in May, 1874, and receiving the degree of Bachelor of Laws. Prof. Dwight speaks of him as follows:

"While in the law school, he was distinguished for the qualities fitting him to be a successful lawyer. He showed a very clear and discriminating mind, apt to learn, ability to grasp and solve knotty legal questions, thoroughness in preparation, and great self-possession and self-control. He was greatly esteemed by his instructors and classmates, and graduated with high distinction. I always looked for great success on his part in the profession, and have not the smallest doubt that had he remained in it he would have reached its highest positions. Having, among his other qualities, an eminently practical mind, he became at an early day versed in railroad questions, while his advice and counsel were eagerly sought for and valued highly. From Mr. Fowler's natural ability, legal acquirements, and sound judgment I do not believe that there are many men in the country better fitted to conduct one of our great railroad enterprises more honorably and successfully than he."

Since his admission to practice, few members of the New York Bar have been so successful in the commercial branch of their profession. Mr. Fowler has been prominently identified with a large number of cases. He has personally conducted intricate legal matters and negotiations for the late William H. Vanderbilt and other distinguished Americans. He is known also to have rendered legal services for James McHenry. Henry Labouchere, and Edmund Yates, of London, England, as well as for leading continental capitalists.

Mr. Fowler was employed by President Gowen, of the Philadelphia and Reading, in many legal struggles with the New Jersey Central Company, and other corporations. Also by the late President Devereux, of the Cleveland, Columbus, Cincinnati and Indianapolis Railroad. In all these important suits he has shown the possession of qualifications which have won him an enviable reputation for professional efficiency.

In 1881 Mr. Fowler was elected Director of the Shenango and Alleghany Railroad. In 1884 we find him a Director of the West Pennsylvania and Shenango Connecting Railroads. On March 15th, of the same year, he was appointed Receiver of the Shenango and Alleghany Railroad and the Mercer Coal and Iron Company. On March 31st following, Mr. Fowler was elected Director of the New York, Ontario and Western Railroad. In 1886 he was elected President. He has also served as Director in the Boards of the East Tennessee, Virginia and Georgia Railroad, and other corporations. No higher tribute could be paid to anyone than the following, which is taken from the Report of R. B. Carnahan, Master of the United States Circuit Court, on the management of the Shenango and Alleghany Railroad by Mr. Fowler as Receiver :

" The duties of the Receiver are laborious, responsible, and require the exercise not only of care and good judgment in the management of the railroad and property, but of unusual caution and tact in the circumstances in which the Receiver was placed, and by which the property was surrounded. All the evidence in the case has satisfied the Master that the operations of the railroad and management of the property of the defendant company were conducted with skill, ability, energy, and good judgment. The Special Master is satisfied, and has found above that the Receiver has discharged the duties of his trust with ability, skill, and fidelity, and no one is found or comes forward alleging the contrary."

The intelligence and fidelity which Mr. Fowler has shown in his various positions, reinforced by the experience gained therein, will doubtless carry him to a much higher one in the railroad world. Standing as he is on the very threshold of his career, he can but feel an honorable degree of pride in the importance and responsibility of the duties now devolving upon him as Chief Executive Officer of the New York, Ontario and Western. Mr. Fowler occupied his country place, in the village of Warwick, during the summer months. In 1876 he married Isabelle, eldest daughter of Benjamin F. Dunning, an eminent New York lawyer, and for many years a partner of Charles O'Conor.

GEORGE M. PULLMAN.

QUITE recently a newspaper correspondent told of his first ride in a sleeping-car. It was in 1859, and among those who took the train with him at Harrisburg, Pa., were Stephen A. Douglas and his wife. All were bound for Chicago, and the sleeping-car was known as No. 29. Mrs. Douglas, like most of her fellow-travelers on that night, had never been in a sleeping-car before, for they had only been running for three or four months and, for the most part, on one or two Western roads. Mrs. Douglas was not overwhelmed by the luxurious comfort of her surroundings, and if we of to-day could see the ramshackle, jingling old ark in which she passed that night on the way home to Chicago, we surely would not charge her discontent to any affected fastidiousness. Imagine an old-fashioned passenger car with the insides torn out of it and in their place two long benches running lengthwise of the car. The only modern survivals sufficiently wretched to be compared with it are some of the side-seated concerns which lurch and wobble up and down the Harlem and New Haven roads to suburban places. Only, even these last venerable survivals of primitive railway development are quite agreeable vehicles compared to the dingy, dimly-lighted sleeping-car of the year before the war. The real misery in those cars was not when you sat sideways and alternately slid into your neighbor's lap and on to the floor. The real suffering began when you turned in for what the Truthful Jameses of the advertising department in those days termed "your luxurious night's repose." The sleeping-car of 1859, when the berths were made up at night, was a sort of combination of the worst features of the Black Hole of Calcutta and the hold of an African slaver. The berths were made up in three-decker style, one above the other, from the floor to within a few inches of the roof of the car. The beds were macadamized mattresses—sheets there were none, pillows there were none. You had a blanket to cover yourself with, and a greasy, shiny haircloth bolster to lay your head on. To slide in between those shelves and to slide out from among your neighbor's lap and on to the floor required the skill of a contortionist. You could have a single berth to yourself by paying one dollar, or you could pay fifty cents and take in lodgers. It is told of Abraham Lincoln that he always paid his fifty cents for a quarter of what is now a section, or half a berth, and that he was never troubled with lodgers, because he was so tall he had to lie diagonally across the bed.

STANDARD ORDER BLANK USED BY MEMBERS OF THE NATIONAL LEAGUE.

JOURNAL

SALESMEN
MUST ENTER HERE
NO. ....

PAGE

SALESMEN MUST USE TWO LINES FOR DESCRIPTION WHERE ONE IS INSUFFICIENT.

SIZES

DESCRIPTION

THE PRESS OF NEW YORK ITS FUTURE.

BY FRANKLIN FORD.

THE future of New York journalism is that of journalism itself. The moving realities of the business must first head up at the metropolis of America. It was there that the new machines of the century, the locomotive and the electric wire, were first brought into full use for newsgathering. The enterprise of the elder Bennett was a clear step forward. Then followed the New York Associated Press, organized to divide the cost of news transmission when telegraphing was expensive. The cost of telegraphing has now fallen so low that it is no longer a hindrance to the freest action. Telegraph charges to the great newspaper are today no more than the postage stamp to the individual. With the discovery of this fact, a new departure in journalism becomes possible.

The newspaper has now at its service an efficient machine. The long-distance telephone marks the completion of this new machine. The next step was to set about organizing the commodity in which the newspaper deals—intelligence. To do this is to get and publish the truth about all sides of human affairs. The more truth the more news, and the more news the greater the profit. The newspapers want this, but are coming to see that the end can only be reached by raising the quality of their goods.

News thus disclosed as commodity is to follow the law of all other commodities, that is, toward improvement in quality with consequent wider consumption. Back in the 70's the people wanted better kerosene. The Standard Oil Company furnished it. The result was a centralized industry, gradually increased consumption of goods, and lower prices. The publishing business has got to go through the same movement. In effecting this the distinction between news and "editorial" will be lost. There is only news—the new thing. The whole publishing business is to be raised to the NEWS idea. The so-called book business is speedily to become secondary or accessory to the daily newspaper.

In this New York is to take the lead. Were the movement to originate in the heart of the country, which is not unlikely, it could only be done in relation to New York. The historian Freeman, in one of his lectures a few years ago, declared that the world had come to be Romeless, that it was without a center. "No longer," he wrote, "does an undivided world look to a single Rome as its one undoubted head. The great feature of the most modern times . . . is the absence of any such center as the world so long gathered itself around." New York is the future Rome, for, in the fullness of electric transmission, it is to become the clearing house of the world's intelligence. In the newer commerce, now fast gathering force, New York is center. A remarkable thing is the fact that the world's intelligence is to be centered and coordinated by English-speaking men.

The multiplication of daily newspapers at New York came about through the premium placed on opinion. When the whole fact was inaccessible, this and that paper was able to sell what some one merely thought was the fact. That day has passed away with the incoming of more complete access. The daily newspaper of the future will replace editorial writing with the skillful and full report. New York will do this first. Once done, the need for half a dozen deliveries of the purported fact will have disappeared.

The change will compel a deal of preparation, but numbers of men must already be working at it. On the one hand, the scientific center is to be erected; on the other, the country will be reported. The one central establishment will take account of the three sides, and, therefore, three profits, which all news presents. For two of these sides, or profits, the trade or class papers, and the "mercantile agencies," stand.

To effect all this, the country will be divided into districts, the manager of each district to draw his salary from New York. The one organization will collect all news, selling its goods through the daily newspaper, the class paper, and the bureau of information. Concerns like the Bradstreet Company and Dun & Company mark the beginnings of the last named.

The changes pending in journalism, and, therefore, in the publishing business as a whole, will be as profound as those following upon the iron business in consequence of Sir Henry Bessemer's steel-making formula. The late postmaster of New York, Henry G. Pearson, was a close student as to the direction of the social forces. He used to say that the present post-office is about completed; that the world must have a new one. This new one he called the spiritual post-office, or the great organic, centralized publishing business. "Down at our place," Pearson would say, "we are arrested if we open a letter. In the post-office that is to be, the arrest will be for failing to open them." He believed that the thought of the people was to find registration.

D. G. Croly, one time managing editor of the New York *World*, but now gathered to his fathers, insisted that "journalism has a theory and a practice which it is desirable to reduce to form." He was, of course, right. In thus insisting, Croly thought himself "first in this country." "A correct theory is the first step towards improvement, by showing what we need and what we might accomplish." The theory of journalism can be nothing short of the science of politics, making the central principle in the light of which the facts are to be organized. The newspaper is nothing by itself, being only the existing organization of intelligence, or lack of it. The newspaper, at any given date, simply reflects prevailing notions. To change it means the working out of advanced methods of reading the social life. The advance can be gained only through the unification of the ideas swarming from the new conditions of life. The ordering of these ideas and their application to reporting as indicated, is to compel a change in the newspaper which can only be compared to the advance of the printing press of to-day over the old Washington hand press.

Horace Greeley once said that the time was coming when all matter for the newspapers would proceed from a single institution. What Greeley did not see is that this one institution must itself be the great central publishing business, handling all news, and, working in relation with the leading paper at each news center of the country, constituting the ultimate associated press.

It is to be understood that the newspaper takes to itself the central position in life. The separation between church and life—making the lesion in the state—which has so perplexed the minds of men, is to disappear. In this respect we revert to the Grecian type of citizenship, the religious and civic merging in the one life of action. A new and prolific unity is dawning in the birth of the Organic State here foreshadowed.

THE TRAVELERS AND THE WORLD'S FAIR.

IN the long marches and conquests of the human race around the world, there is one historical fact in the grandeur and magnitude of its results that stands unapproached since the morning of the creation. At a distance of four hundred years from that single event, and over four thousand miles from the little seaport town of Palos, in Andalusia, from which the Genoese navigator sailed on a memorable Friday morning in 1492, the nations of the earth are to join in the celebration of that unexampled achievement.

It was a discovery that startled the civilized world from a consuming lethargy of a thousand years, lifted the united crowns of Castile and Arragon from poverty to imperial affluence and power, and terminated the history of medieval ages. Over the bright crestline of that one discovery the old nations saw the outlines of a new hemisphere. It inspired their people with a spirit of adventure and enterprise. Never before had a revelation so suddenly quickened a whole continent to activity. It was a new commercial and industrial birth, stupendous and immeasurable in its consequences. Not a resurrection of old civilization, nor a reproduction of ancient cities with their vain pomp and ceremonials, but the vigorous growth of a new existence, in the light of an electric spark and upon the exhaustless power of compressed vapor.

Following the example of the great discoverer, adventurers from Spain penetrated Mexico and formed a settlement at San Augustine, upon the peninsula of Florida. French navigators invaded Canada and the northern lakes in their voyages of discovery. The cavaliers of England made a settlement at Jamestown, Virginia; the Puritan took possession of the Plymouth Colony; the brotherly Quakers found a hospitable lodgment at Philadelphia, and the Dutch merchant established his trading-post on Manhattan Island. Emigration from all climes and countries poured in upon the eastern coast of the North American continent.

Comparatively few Americans probably realize the importance that the colonization of America, and the experiences of the independent nations subsequently formed here, have assumed in the minds of the social thinkers, of the political thinkers, and of the political leaders of Europe. In remembering what these things mean to us, we have been apt to forget what these things have meant to them. Steadily the primary significance and the proper consequences of the discovery of America have grown in the estimation of the great minds of the Old World, and even in popular thought there; while, of late, the influence of American ideas and American institutions upon the policies and the industries of Europe, has risen to a maximum.

The highest civilization has always been achieved by commercial people. Scholars, philosophers, and reformers have always been regarded as valuable to the state, but they are never builders. They construct ideals and theories, while the necessities of commerce and trade not only determine governmental policies, but erect proud cities, establish long lines of traffic, teach the arts through invention, add new forces to progress, and civilize mankind with electricity. It is the commerce of a nation, therefore, that best measures its advancement and greatness.

The greatest work of the Exposition will be to widen the markets for products, through educating the taste of consumers and inspiring industrial ambitions. It is in pressing for new ends, in setting up larger and finer objects of desire, that an exhibition of arts and manufactures chiefly contributes to industrial development. In addition, Chicago affords the largest opportunity for a gathering of people of widely sundered sections, that is as much to be desired for its social and political effects.

The citizens of the Southern and Northwestern States will pour into Chicago to visit the Exposition, in throngs that will long remain the subject of wonder and admiration. And the population that will be brought within the reach of these educating and inspiring influences will be such as it is preëminently desirable to reach and to affect. It will consist largely of those who usually have little opportunity for indulging themselves in recreation, and small privileges for the cultivation of the finer tastes of life.

The commercial traveler takes in all the rubrics of the practice of the arts and trades, of agriculture, of commerce, and of the arts of design. He believes in the display of ideas; of comparison on a grand scale; of the novel and extraordinary. He it is who appreciates that the march of time is unceasing and productive of uncertain results. He knows that experience forbids us to look upon any human conception as immutable. Great merchant princes and the most successful men have been commercial travelers in their day.

The two hundred thousand commercial travelers of this country control the trade of the continent. They alone can prevent the formation of trusts by the maintenance of prices for products, and thus solve the problem of the hour. To solve this problem, either one of two things must be: The producers must be pooled, and this means limitation of production, or the sellers must combine. A combination of the travelers will make them the controlling spirits of the age.

The influences leading forward to the organization of the travelers are worthy of consideration. They embrace the expansion of commerce upon this continent. Without railroads or steamboats, and even without stage coaches, the early commercial travelers of this country pioneered their way beyond the frontier lines of civilization, and established trading posts among the children of the forests.

Through storm and sunshine; over streams and mountainous regions, with no comforts of a hotel or care in sickness, they led the way and staked the lines of the future railway system of the country, over which the great flood of civilization found its way to the dark places of the continent. All these hardships were endured, and undertakings made successful, that the merchant prince might enlarge his trade and augment his fortune.

In the accomplishment of all this he makes a sacrifice of a large portion of his home life and of the society of his wife and children. He sends them his love and salary, but can seldom be with them. He must travel almost without ceasing, at all times of day or night, in good or indifferent conveyances, sleeping and eating with a rush, and either in sickness or health, travel-worn, tired, depressed or hopeful, be the same genial, cordial gentleman always. If discouragement or disappointment overtake him he must not show it, or, if his wife or any of his little ones are ill, he must press the sad news back to his heart, because commerce and trade demand his best efforts.—R. R. F.

THE PENNSYLVANIA ◦ RAILROAD ◦ COMPANY

TO THE

NATIONAL LEAGUE OF TRAVELERS CLUBS

Greeting:

IT seems almost unnecessary to direct the attention of this Association to the facilities afforded by the Pennsylvania Railroad. The organization is composed of men a part of whose profession is the art of travel. They are shrewd and of discriminating tastes, and it is therefore natural that they should select the best railway line, just as they choose the best hotel in each town on their itinerary. The Pennsylvania Railroad is by universal consent the "Standard Railroad of America," and as such it appeals to the consideration of the man who travels for business or pleasure. Its lines are so comprehensive, and its friendly connections so complete, that the majority of the cities and towns in the Union are easily accessible by its superb service of through and local trains.

These trains are equipped with Pullman Vestibule Sleeping Cars, Parlor Cars, and Passenger Coaches, all embodying in their construction and furnishing the latest features which tend to contribute comfort and luxury to travel on the rails. The roadbed is admittedly the best and most substantial, the safety appliances are so complete that they surround the traveler with the most reliable assurances of security.

The rates of fare prevailing on this system are exceedingly reasonable, considering the high grade of service which they embrace. The system of tickets include a range of territory wider in extent than that of any other line, and the conditions under which they are sold are liberal.

These are a few of the advantages which this line presents to the Traveling Men of America. They are so strong as to compel their recognition.

GEO. W. BOYD,   J. R. WOOD,
Asst. G. P. A.   *G. P. A.*

W. A. Power

Musical Director Commercial Travelers Club

Mr. William A. Power was born in Boston thirty-two years ago. His father, Richard Power, has been one of the leading business men in the marble business of that city for forty years, and was formerly a resident of New York City. William graduated at the Boston High School at the age of sixteen, carrying off all the honors. His parents wished him to enter college, but he preferred going with his father in business, with whom he remained for three years. When but a child, he displayed marked aptitude for music, and while still in business, he played for the élite of Boston. At the age of nineteen he went to the Masconomo House, Manchester-by-the-Sea, which is owned by the charming and incomparable actress, Mrs. Agnes Booth. For the last twelve seasons he has had charge of the music at that place. During the winter season he kept up his entertainments with the leading families of Boston. For the past two years he has been in New York City, following his profession. Mr. Power has played with approval before the following people, the mention of whose names will remain, not only the best indorsement, but the brightest reminiscence of Mr. Power's career: Ward McAllister, Mrs. Walter Cutting, Mrs. P. Morgan, Mrs. Richard M. Hunt, Mrs. Bradley Martin, Mrs. John Jacob Astor. After the first night at which he was engaged by The Commercial Travelers Club, they made him Musical Director, a position which he has held ever since. He is a musical genius. May he live long and prosper.

JNO. B. BLACK

BROTHERHOOD OF COMMERCIAL TRAVELERS
EIGHTH ANNUAL BANQUET.

The "American Stationer" of December 20, 1892.

HE Brotherhood of Commercial Travelers held its eighth annual banquet last night at the Hotel Marlborough, and it was an enjoyable and successful affair.

President John H. Black presided and was flanked on the right by Will Carleton, James Clarence Hervey, ex-President Col. J. H. Ammon, ex-President J. A. McQuillan, and Captain Wiams, and on the left by ex-Governor Waller of Connecticut, ex-President, J. F. Hitchcock, ex-President William J. Kelly, G. W. Proctor Knott, President Commercial Travelers' Club, and Secretary John Hovendon. Among those who graced the other tables were Messrs. James T. Watkins, A. D. McMullen, J. L. Marony, Tremain, Fitzgerald, Samuel Eckstein, C. W. Cook, J. M. Tate, C. T. Dillingham, G. W. Dillingham, J. A. Holden, Metcalf, A. H. Berrell, C. Henry, John Bacon Moser, E. L. McDonald, Paul Latham, William Jarchow, E. E. Besser, Sam Jesselson, Captain Mandeville, G. W. Hills, E. C. Carroll, A. S. Willdigg, Bert. Caldwell, Liddell, J. Magee, A. E. Turner, John Ryan, V. M. Coryell, I. M. Loughead, B. E. Pike, McInnes, R. F. Fenno, Dwight Terry, F. A. Coombs, S. Vander Wheeden, Wagner, Lawrence Manning, J. L. Peebles, J. G. Hart, Homer P. Beach, J. L. Shepherd, S. L. McGonigal, Jonas Langfeld.

When coffee was reached President Black rapped for order and called on J. F. Hitchcock, who read some letters of regret. A telegram was also received from G. A. Ayres.

President Black then introduced James Clarence Hervey, who in a very clever, happy way made a brief speech and told a couple of witty stories.

John G. Hart, vice-president of the Commercial Travelers Club, sang "The man who broke the bank at Monte Carlo," and later in the evening the same gentleman favored the company with "The Man in the Moon."

James D. Mandeville, vice-president of the Tenderloin Club, made a speech in which he advocated the consolidation of the Brotherhood of Commercial Travelers and the Commercial Travelers Club. He then referred to the important position held by traveling men. There were 250,000 of them in the United States, and that body of men had done more to represent the industries of the country than all the politicians of the two great parties.

Will Carleton was the next speaker. He said that he supposed he was entitled to be present at a gathering of commercial travelers because he had been on the road selling books. When he made his first attempts in literature he tried to find a publisher, but all to whom he applied referred him to the "fellow just around the corner." He finally went to see Mr. Donnelly of Chicago, and he told him he wanted him to publish a book of poetry. Donnelly looked tired, and it was only when the speaker convinced him by means of the letter S crossed by two upright lines, that he undertook the work. The speaker said that he then became the wholesale dealer, appointed subagents, etc., and finally worked off two or three hundred copies. He then wrote to Donnelly for more, but that gentleman said that the edition was exhausted, and when asked to explain, said: "We had a fire the other day, and the edition is all gone." Mr. Carleton then referred to the great advance which had been made in these latter days, and said that publishers could get along without the author, as they could go on putting forth the works of the fellows who were dead. The publisher, however, was very necessary to the author. In closing, Mr. Carleton recited one of his own poems, "The Christmas Baby," which was applauded to the echo.

Ex-Governor Waller of Connecticut made a brief address, in opening which he said that President Black and he were old shipmates, if not old salts. They had crossed the ocean together, and President Black was the life of the ship, as he was one of those happy mortals who was always sunshine. The speaker brought himself into the ranks of the poets by telling of his early efforts in constructing verse. He also said that he had had relations with publishers, for a local poet in his State wrote a poem which ran:

> And for Waller we will holler,
> He is poet, statesman, scholar,
> And one of the boys.

This poet afterward published a book of his work, but the speaker after buying one of the volumes was disappointed to find that this gem was omitted.

Mr. Waller paid a compliment to the energy and industry of commercial travelers, and said that it was one of the pleasures of his life that in his travels he had been able to meet the business men of this and other countries. In closing, the speaker called on the company to drink to the health of the B. C. T. and of President Black. The company did.

Lawrence Manning, of the Maude Granger Company, told in verse the story of "The Tramp," and as an encore gave "Spartacus' Address." His work was excellent and won hearty rounds of applause.

John L. Shepherd told some good stories, and then called the attention of those present to the impositions which were practiced on travelers. He said that travelers must remember that employers were given to figuring expenses in salaries, and that reduced expenses meant increased salaries. He said by united action the imposition by railroads and hotels could be remedied.

G. W. Proctor Knott spoke for the Commercial Travelers Club. He gave a history of the organization, showing that it was started by six men a year ago last Thanksgiving Day, and that since that time it had a phenomenal growth. It hoped soon to erect a clubhouse of its own, although its present quarters were equipped in first-class style in every respect. He advocated the consolidation of the two organizations, and on behalf of the Commercial Travelers Club offered the members of the Brotherhood of Commercial Travelers the hospitality of his club. In New York there were 116,000 traveling men, and there was every reason why those men should have for themselves the finest clubhouse in America.

F. A. RINGLER & CO.,
MANUFACTURERS OF
PLATES FOR ALL PRINTING PURPOSES BY VARIOUS PROCESSES,
21 & 23 Barclay St., to 26 and 28 Park Place, New York.

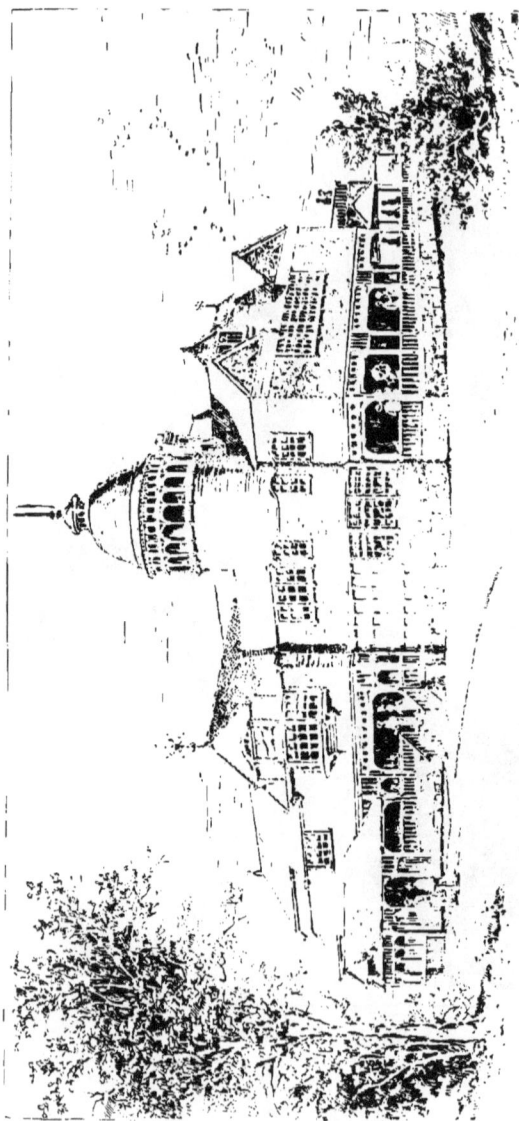

AMERICAN YACHT CLUB ON LONG ISLAND SOUND.

B. BROWNE'S

MESSAGE

TO THE GREAT ADVERTISERS OF

AMERICA.

THE importance of Great Britain and her possessions as profitable markets for American productions, popularized by advertising, has never yet been realized by the great advertisers of America.

With Free Trade, and almost free freights, business intercourse between the two countries is actually easier than between New York and most other American cities.

The establishment of my New York offices affords the opportunity to those interested in the subject, of being placed in immediate touch with an organization embracing the entire press of Great Britain, Australia, South Africa and India.

A vast experience gained in handling the announcements of the world's most successful advertisers is at the service of intending clients.

A personal call, to inspect the files of English and Colonial Newspapers, or correspondence invited.

BROWNE,

161 AND 163 QUEEN VICTORIA STREET, LONDON, ENG.

AND 353 AND 355 CANAL STREET, NEW YORK.

PHOTOGRAPHED BY FALK

REPRESENTATIVE FINANCIERS OF THE UNITED STATES.

JOSEPH W. REINHART.

The reorganization of the Atchison, Topeka & Santa Fé Railroad, and the placing of the system upon a substantial and enduring basis, stand as a perpetual monument to the consummate skill, indomitable energy, superior business tact, and unsurpassed diplomacy in the railroad world, of one man. That man is Mr. Joseph W. Reinhart, who was recently placed at the head of the company by his election to the presidency. A more fitting tribute to honors earned, a more just recognition of services rendered, or greater wisdom in the selection of the man for the place, has never been exhibited in this country.

The Atchison system, as it exists to-day, has a greater mileage than that of any other railroad system in the United States, or, for that matter, in the world. A few years ago—the other day, so to speak—the company was hopelessly bankrupt. With the numerous and in many respects conflicting interests involved, with different classes of bonds secured by separate mortgages on different sections of the system, and with their complex and imperfectly defined relations to each other and to the parent company, foreclosure and sale under the auctioneer's hammer seemed inevitable. Such was the opinion of the leading financial doctors of the country who carefully diagnosed the case.

But without foreclosure, without the dismemberment of the system or the loss of any of its component parts, the Atchison has been reorganized upon a basis that insures a low rate of fixed charges, together with an ample supply of funds to meet extraordinary expenditures for additions and improvements for years to come without encroaching upon the current traffic revenues. The aggregate mileage operated is now much greater than it was before reorganization, and the different sections have been firmly and securely knit together into a compact whole, forming one of the most perfect railroad systems in the country. In a word, the Atchison system of to-day is invulnerable from a financial standpoint, while under its enlarged reorganization, it spans the continent from the Great Lakes to the Pacific Ocean, traversing some of the richest sections of that broad belt known as the Great Mississippi Valley, and bringing to the doors of millions of people quick transit for themselves and their merchandise to the centers of the commercial world.

Like all other American railroad monarchs, Mr. Reinhart is a self-made man—he has climbed the full length of the ladder from the bottom rung, and is, therefore, entitled to all the honors that may be bestowed upon him. His first important step upward was taken when he advanced from superintendent's clerk of the Allegheny Valley Railroad to the position of Superintendent of Transportation of the same line. Then he became Auditor of the Richmond and Allegheny Railroad and the James River Canal and Richmond Dock Companies. Later on we find him General Auditor of the West Shore Railroad. That was before the company was placed

PHOTOGRAPHED BY FALK

in receivers' hands, but he continued to hold the same position as long as the court had charge of the property, and until it was transferred to the New York Central.

Mr. Reinhart began his official relations with the Atchison as General Auditor of the system, and subsequently, under the reorganization, he was made Vice-President and General Auditor, which offices he continued to hold until his recent election to the presidency of the company. But during all the time that the work of financial rehabilitation was under way, his was the master-mind that conducted the company safely through the labyrinthian complications in which it had become involved; and since that gigantic work was completed, the same hand has led it in its further work of extension and development, until, as stated above, the Atchison system stands without its equal in this or any other country.

JAY GOULD.

Mr. Jay Gould was a great man.

It is difficult, so soon after his death, to present a definitive estimate of this extraordinary individuality. There are many who, having challenged him to battle, found themselves defeated; others, who were willing to speculate freely and incur risks so long as there was prospect of great profit, who lost and laid the blame at the door of Jay Gould. These, and a certain portion of the snarleyow press, willfully closed their eyes to the fact that men who go to battle ought to expect to fight, and that in all fights one side must suffer defeat. Jay Gould had many defeats in life, but he bore them like a man, bided his time, and did his best to secure the perchment of victory upon his banners in subsequent encounters. The story of his experiences reads like a romance, yet it was stern reality with him, every move being the result of thought, every step in accordance with programme. Although delicate

in physique Mr. Gould had an immensity of nerve fiber, which enabled him to endure long spells of mental fatigue without physical breakdown. Obviously, that course could not be pursued with safety beyond a certain age, and his death at a comparatively youthful term is the best possible proof of that assertion. Although Mr. Gould was educated to be a surveyor, his field of operations was too wide to be bounded by ordinary chain, or measured by regulation rod. The little village in which he was born was not adapted in its metes and bounds to his comfortable existence, so he sought the imperial metropolis, where men of mental might and financial strength, and widespread ambitions, were his neighbors and his competitors.

He had no rivals.

Rivalry can exist only between equals. One would as soon think of rivalry between an ordinary car-horse and Maud S., as between the ordinary financier and Jay Gould. In characterizing such an entity as he, one looks in vain for comparisons. It is only by contrasts that he can be properly judged. Jay Gould had a subtle sense of humor peculiarly his own. It gratified him immensely to pit his brain against the combined strength of thousands, to outmaneuver, to outgeneral, to defeat them. He was secretive, because secrecy was a prime essential in the successful carrying out of financial programmes. A distinguished lawyer once said that in all the famous Erie litigation Jay Gould never lost a point, because his counsel showed him the bearing of the laws, and his own superintelligence suggested to him not only the safety but the wisdom of confining all his operations within the boundaries laid down by the makers of the statutes, adding, "Gould would have made one of our greatest lawyers." That he was beyond all possibility of challenge the greatest financier America ever knew, is so universally conceded that further exploiture is unnecessary.

But he was more than that.

Geo. B. Valente

The story of his home as told by his children, the record of his unvarying courtesy and generosity as disclosed by the testimony of his employees, revealed Jay Gould's character in a light so different from that which the unthinking and at times unfairly censorious public know of, as to be positively amazing. The affection which existed between him and his children, and notably with his eldest son, who was his constant companion and most intimate friend, amounted almost to a passion. His refined and gentle nature found most enjoyable pleasure amid the beauties and the glories and the extraordinary developments of his conservatories and hothouses. All that was simple and domestic, and, if the phrase may be used, hearthstony in life, had for him peculiar attractions, and his chief comfort and solace and balm and soothing influence in times of disturbance, anxiety, and positive distress, were found either in the pleasant retiracies of his home in the city, or in the calm and quiet solitudes of his magnificent place upon the Hudson. Dying, at what would seem an unusually and unfortunately early age, Jay Gould left many millions, indeed, but, better than that, he also left many appreciative, kindly thinking, warmly approving friends.

GEORGE J. GOULD.

Mr. Jay Gould was a student of human nature.

In fact, it may be said he was a professor in the college of human nature. He understood men thoroughly. His judgment of the mental, moral, physical, executive qualities of subordinates was remarkable. Five years before his death he selected George J. Gould, his eldest son, as his *alter ego*, placing upon his young shoulders a heavy burden, the responsibility of which ordinary men need not hope to understand, much less appreciate. After five years' closest intimacy, during which the senior Gould had ample opportunity to study the young

man, to weigh him, and estimate his character, he emphasized the wisdom of his original selection by intrusting him, by the terms of his will, with the virtual management of his vast estate, and bequeathing to him, with a touch of humor which was eminently characteristic of the late financier, five millions of dollars in payment for his services during the five years referred to.

That's a proud record.

George J. Gould is entitled by provable facts to regard himself as a dutiful son, a trusted employee, a man of unusual brainific gift. The testimony of Jay Gould, the father, is quite sufficient to prove the first. Surely no father ever needed the close companionship, the charming comradeship, the trusty arm of a well-beloved son, more absolutely than he. Marvelously gifted himself in the mental stratum, he was physically weak. In this respect his son differed from him, for the early training of George Gould was that of an athlete. Outdoor sports and all manner of physical developing recreation were his delight, and he developed when yet a very young man a sturdiness of stamina which has stood him in good stead in many an hour of anxious thought and many a period of wearing solicitude. Upon this son's arm Jay Gould rested absolutely. Having tested him along the lines of *morale*, knowing that nothing could swerve him in his loyalty to his father's interests, he left time and again his tremendous interests in the hands of one who appeared to many, ere they dealt with him, but a lad. The lad, however, was the father's son, and there is no doubt that the absolute confidence manifested by the father was a seed sown in fallow ground, ultimately bearing a great harvest of reciprocal regard, born not at all of greed, avarice, or special interest, but rather of honest love for a generous and a confiding parent.

This trust was a compliment.

Nothing stimulates, in generous natures, a determination to be zealous in the best interests of an employer, so much as perfect confidence. One's

FRANK THOMPSON

motto instantly becomes *noblesse oblige*, and from that moment confidence is well bestowed, trust is well placed, for loyalty is at the helm, and the desired haven will be made, if brains and care and industry intelligently directed can effect that purpose.

Obviously, then, the brains are there.

It is fair to assume that however much Jay Gould might have loved his son, however much it would have gratified him to trust him and rested him to lean upon him, he would not have been so recreant to his own interest as to roll his burdens upon George, had he not recognized in him a man of unusual natural ability, with marked aptitude to learn and understand. Men of affairs on " the street," in the parlors of great corporations, recognize in George Gould not only a man worth millions of money, not only a man of ample opportunity, not only one who has had exceptional advantages in training, but a clean-cut American identity, whose desires, aims, and ambitions are, to say the least, abreast with the progress, the enthusiasm, the triumphs of the age, with a head well packed, ideas clearly marked, programmes cleverly laid and definitely placed. Fortunately, accompanying these rare gifts is an expert knowledge of men, considerable caution, a love of equity, and self-respect. To these are added perfect health, a genial manner, a modest bearing, all tinged and made acceptable by an utter absence of purse-pride, arrogance, self-conceit, or jealousy.

GEORGE B. ROBERTS.

Mr. George B. Roberts, Civil Engineer and President of the Pennsylvania Railroad Company, was born in Montgomery County, Pennsylvania, January 15, 1833. Mr. Roberts' early education was received at the Rensselaer Polytechnic Institute at Troy, N. Y., and his entire life since his school days has practically been spent in railroad service. In 1851 he began active railroading as a rodman employed

in the construction of the mountain division of the Pennsylvania Railroad.

In 1852 he became assistant engineer of the Philadelphia and Erie Railroad, and for the subsequent ten years was steadily engaged in the location and construction of various roads, including the Sunbury and Erie, the North Pennsylvania and Western Pennsylvania, the Allentown and Auburn, the Mahanoy and Broad Mountain, the West Jersey, and other roads, many of which were completed by him as chief engineer. In 1862 he returned to the Pennsylvania Railroad with the title of assistant to the president, under J. Edgar Thomson, at that time president of the company. Mr. Roberts' skill as an engineer and his fine administrative abilities marked him for promotion to the fourth vice-presidency in 1869. This election was followed almost immediately by another making him second vice-president. Upon the accession of Colonel Thomas A. Scott to the presidency, June 3, 1874, Mr. Roberts was advanced by him to the first vice-presidency. In this new capacity Mr. Roberts had charge of all engineering matters relating to the construction, extension, and improvement of the company's lines, and a general supervision of the accounts through the comptroller. He also assisted the president with all business connected with other roads leased or controlled by the Pennsylvania Railroad Company. Upon the death of Colonel Scott in 1880, Mr. Roberts became president of the company.

The Pennsylvania Railroad and branches, together with its connections west of Pittsburg and Erie, embrace an aggregate mileage of nearly ten thousand miles running through nine States of the Union. The employees number about 100,000, ranging from the section hand to the keenest financiering and executive talent, including artisans in every conceivable branch of industry, embracing all the arts and professions, and affecting innumerable and widely separated communities. Greater in importance even than this is the relation of the

Horace Porter

road to the country at large. Its stockholders number twenty thousand, and they are scattered over two continents.

Over all, Mr. Roberts is the presiding genius.

FRANK THOMSON.

Mr. Frank Thomson, First Vice-President of the Pennsylvania Railroad, is unquestionably one of the ablest railway managers in the country. Just in the prime of life, he has devoted the entire period from early manhood to the practical study and actual operation of the line on which he now holds so prominent a position. Graduated from Franklin and Marshall College in Pennsylvania at the age of eighteen, he at once secured an engagement in the shops at Altoona, where in the course of several years he became thoroughly grounded in the practical work of constructing locomotives and cars, as well as in the handling of them when placed in active service. With the vast store of knowledge and experience gained in this school he was peculiarly fitted to enter upon the successful career which the future had in store. Promotion came rapidly. From division superintendent he ascended through all the grades of superintendent of motive power, general manager, and second vice-president, to that of first vice-president, which he now holds.

During this time he has not only witnessed the development of the railway system of America, but by his sagacity, judgment, and broad-minded views on all questions, contributed as much as any other living railway man to the development of that high state of efficiency which the American system has reached. His work in the various positions which he has filled on the Pennsylvania Railroad reflects the utmost credit upon his ability. He instituted reforms in the management, administration, and maintenance of the road, which have not only placed the Pennsylvania in the forefront of American railways, but have set the standard for all other lines. The substantial construction of road-bed and bridges, and the maintenance of the line in the highest condition by the award of prizes for the best kept sections of track; the introduction of the block signal and other safety appliances; the building of attractive stations and the ornamentation of their grounds, and the high class of equipment for which the road is celebrated, are to be credited to his genius. He is also endowed with fine administrative and executive abilities, and not only founded but developed the system of discipline which distinguishes the organization of the forces he directs.

Mr. Thomson is thoroughly conversant with every detail of railway affairs, and this knowledge, coupled with his tact, ability, and energy, equips him thoroughly for the responsible duties of his very important office.

GENERAL HORACE PORTER.

It is difficult to photograph so many-sided a man as General Horace Porter. He has so many faces that it is virtually impossible to picture him all at once, yet it would not be entirely safe to speak of him even as a two-faced man. Obviously, then, he is a contradiction. Some there are who think of him as a public poser, an after-dinner speaker, a teller of funny stories; others know him chiefly through his record as one of Grant's military family—the only one, indeed, who appears to have been able to do much in the way of honoring the name and perpetuating the fame of his beloved commander.

But he is more than these.

General Porter has that happiest of faculties, a knowledge of human nature, which enables him to prove himself a square peg in a square hole at all times and under all circumstances. As Vice-President of the Pullman Palace Car Company, and vir-

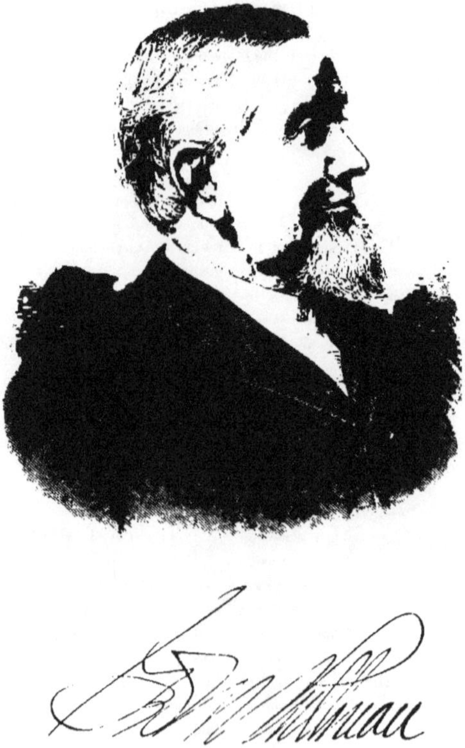

tually its executive chief, his military training is of vast advantage to the great corporation, part of which he is. He controls with apparent ease, and certainly without evidences of mental, moral, or physical fatigue, a multitude of employés, clerks, conductors, porters, masters of transportation, agents of various name, involving a familiarity with the tendencies of mankind in general and the peculiarities of railroad officials in particular. The manipulation of the affairs of his corporation brings him into close contact and frequent intercourse with men of large affairs, where again he is found entirely competent to deal with questions of wide-scoped interest, and with men sometimes narrow-minded, pig-headed, obstinate, and perverse.

He is a man of boundless energy.

No better illustration of this could be asked than the success which he compelled in respect of the long-delayed monument to General Grant. It is not to the credit of the American people, but it is a fact, nevertheless, that the public did not respond to the call made by the Memorial Committee. It would be useless to analyze the reasons for this. That they existed was painfully evident. Stung to the quick by what was not only national ingratitude but a blot upon the fair fame of the Republic, General Porter, single-handed and alone, resolved that that monument fund should be raised. It is matter of record that he bombarded the newspapers with bulletins, circulated leaflets among the people like snowflakes, made addresses all over the city, three or four in an evening, threw himself with the velocity of an electric projectile against rich men, common men, corporations, and other holders of the great American dollar, until at last, on one bright October day, it was his proud privilege to announce that the fund was finished and not another dollar needed.

Obviously, then, he is popular.

The community wouldn't have tolerated from many men such incisive arguments, such contemptuous rakings over, as made the Porterian utterance luminous and effective. His popularity is further attested by the fact that when the genial and effervescent Chauncey M. Depew gracefully retired from the presidency of the Union League Club, General Porter was the unanimous choice to that proud social pre-eminence. No speaker is more warmly welcomed anywhere, everywhere, than this same deservedly popular individuality, General Horace Porter.

JOHN W. MACKAY.

Of all the sturdy Irish-American lads who have risen to fame, and deserved repute of wide horizon, none stands higher than John W. Mackay of California, New York, and the world in general.

He is unique.

Possessed of wealth, which a quarter of a century ago would have been deemed fabulous, standing among the very rich men of the earth, he is the same clear-eyed, warm-hearted, open-handed John he was "way back" in the fifties. Old-time miners speak of him as a man of grit, pluck, personal courage, and strict integrity. What his poker qualifications are, may be a question, but no tough ever succeeded in bluffing him in private life. The jury of the vicinage is what we look to when we seek a significant verdict, and it is the unanimous verdict of California miners, that the word of John W. Mackay was as good as anybody else's bond, and subsequently as good as any issue of his own. It is easy enough for men with millions to be honest, but Mackay's reputation in that line was based upon his universally recognized character long before the "pocket" was opened or the metal gave a "show."

And so everywhere.

The character he made and the reputation he enjoyed among his comrades in the olden times,

ENGRAVED ON M & PLCENT PHOTOGRAPH

JOHN WILLIAM MACKAY.

attend him now that his associates are the great factors in the busy, restless life of commerce, and, indeed, in the higher realms of scientific development. It is not, however, as a man of money his friends most highly regard him. He is comradic and fraternal. He is considerate and thoughtful, he is generosity itself. It is well known that he was one of the twenty-five thousand dollar subscribers to the two hundred and fifty thousand dollar fund raised for that maker of history, Ulysses S. Grant. It is not known, however, by the general public that he offered to be one of ten, and subsequently one of five, to raise a fund of a million dollars for the well-styled savior of the Union. Pursued by sharpers, besieged by adventurers, sought by great names in finance, tempted by commercial magnates, Mr. Mackay never loses his head, but pursues the even tenor of his way, utterly unaffected, and surely without affectation or ostentation, ever mindful that the highest happiness is enjoyed by men who are true to themselves, as well as honest in dealing with their fellows.

GENERAL THOMAS T. ECKERT.

General Thomas T. Eckert has been known for years by capitalists, journalists, electricians, and telegraphers as a man of unusual natural gifts, and with rare executive ability. In the prime of life he stands at the head of the greatest organization in the world. As President of the Western Union Telegraph Company, he is identified with the management of corporate assets worth scores of millions of dollars. He is the target for every scientific thinker. His acquiescence is the Mecca toward which every electrician of an inventive turn of mind tends. He is in command of an army of men and women, not less than twenty thousand strong, and this army has in it many thousands who

are superintelligent, industrious, trustworthy, and expert.

How did he get there?

That's the kind of greatness which is not thrust upon one, but is honestly earned, worthily gained, and if, in addition thereto, it is modestly worn and all aroundedly controlled, he who has it is indeed envied among his fellows. General Eckert fills that bill absolutely. His entire life, intelligently industrious, has been devoted to the interests of telegraphy, and that means the interest of humanity. Without the telegraph, nations would be in the dark as to the progress and intentions each of the other. The peoples of the earth would be densely ignorant, as compared with their enlightenment of today. We who use the telegraphic wire as in olden times men used the stage-coach, rarely stop to think what that universal convenience means. A moment's reflection furnishes a photograph of the situation as it is, and a suggestion of what it would be were telegraphic communication no longer possible.

In some respects General Eckert is a genius.

During the late Civil War the National Government, recognizing his ability, conscious of his integrity, and fortunate in his loyalty, leaned upon him in times of emergency with justifiable heaviness. The Government's confidence was never betrayed. Its best interests were always consulted, and its appreciation of one of its most valued aids was fully manifested. In many respects General Eckert differs from his predecessors. Mr. Orton was a diplomat. Dr. Norvin Green was a specialist, in that he was master of the art of conviction, having few, if any, equals as a debater and explainer, an advocate in the presence of legislative committee or directorate board. Although fully familiar with the technique of telegraphy, and well acquainted with the lay of this great land, over which the network of the Western Union's wires is so deftly placed, General Eckert comes to the front at a time when a clear

Thos. T. Eckert.

head and a firm disciplinary hand are the great desiderata. It may well be doubted if any widespread dissatisfaction will be found in the Western Union's army, while Eckert is in command. There will be no significant strikes, no interruption to this chief public convenience, no unsettlable trouble with authorities, but the dead level of expert management will be maintained, and held in perfect control by one who is a man among men, quick to detect fraud and imposition, but ever ready to recognize and appreciate honest service, professional merit, and scientific progress.

MR. CHARLES KING LORD.

While in Baltimore recently, a commercial traveler had occasion to call on business at the big Baltimore and Ohio building, where the affairs of this huge railroad corporation are directed. He was ushered into the presence of the Third Vice-President, Mr. C. K. Lord, on the second floor, and did not have to warm his heels very long, either, before he got an audience. He found Mr. Lord a typical railroad man—pleasant, affable, polite, direct in his inquiries, and business-like in every respect. Even the office boy, who brought him his mail, and the colored porter, who dusted his table, received the kindliest expressions from him. The visiting traveler was led to inquire something about such a man—a man who has as many good things said about him as any other man in Baltimore. Everybody knows him, and everybody

likes him. If he had been a commercial traveler —well, he would have made the boys hustle for business all the way from New York to San Francisco. He knows all the intricacies of railroad management, and is probably the only man who has been in the service of any of the Trunk lines, who has been promoted from the position of General Passenger Agent to that of Vice-President—a promotion which was won solely upon merit. Mr. Lord is a native of New York State, having been born at Hoosac Falls, May 14, 1848. He entered the railway service Oct. 1, 1865. In 1871 he was a clerk in the general ticket office of the Indianapolis, Cincinnati and La Fayette Railroad. In six months he was general ticket agent of the same road. From April 1, 1873, until Oct., 1874, he was its Assistant General Passenger Agent. In 1874 he was made General Passenger and Ticket Agent, which position he resigned in 1874 to become General Passenger Agent of the St. Louis, Kansas City and Northern Railway. He served in this capacity until 1879, when he accepted the post of General Ticket Agent of the Wabash, St. Louis and Pacific road. A year later he entered the service of the Baltimore and Ohio Company as General Passenger Agent. Eight years later, in 1888, he was elected to the Third Vice-Presidency. He organized the passenger department of the Baltimore and Ohio. Mr. Charles O. Scull, the incumbent General Passenger Agent, has been a most worthy successor. Mr. Lord has a charming home in North Baltimore, the fashionable section of the city, presided over by a charming wife. He has one son, now a college student, and two daughters.

MR. CHARLES KING LORD.

JOSEPH W. REINHART.

President Atchison, Topeka & Santa Fe R. R. Company.

A. A. McLEOD,

THE OLDEST AND FOREMOST PASSENGER-CARRYING RAILROAD OF THE WORLD.

WITHIN a few years wonderful progress has been made in enhancing the comforts of travelers. It is characteristic of this country that the oldest railroad corporation in America should have taken the lead in this advance.

The Baltimore and Ohio Railroad was the first passenger-carrying road in America, and it continues to be one of the most popular routes of travel from the Atlantic coast to the great West, *via* Washington. The Baltimore and Ohio Railroad was also the first railroad to respond to the popular demand for faster train service, and, in connection with the Central Railroad of New Jersey and the Philadelphia and Reading Railroad, established the famous Royal Blue Line train-service between New York, Philadelphia, Baltimore, and Washington. All these trains are equipped with the finest and safest passenger cars ever constructed. They were built especially for the line at the celebrated shops of the Pullman Company, at Pullman, Ill. They are provided with Pullman patent safety vestibules and with Pullman's anti-telescoping device; they are heated by steam and lighted by Pintsch gas. Separate retiring and toilet rooms are provided in each car for ladies and gentlemen, in addition to which each car contains a smoking compartment with sofa-seats and movable chairs for the accommodation of lovers of the weed. The Royal Blue Line Limited was the first regular passenger train ever scheduled at so high a rate of speed, and its successful performance has demonstrated to railway managers the entire practicability of making fast time compatible with the same degree of safety and accuracy that surrounds the movement of slower trains.

The Royal Blue Limited has reduced the running time between New York and Washington to five hours. The importance of the travel between New York and Washington induced the company to first apply the great improvements outlined above on that branch, but it is only a small part of their vast system. Their lines extend from New York, Philadelphia, and Baltimore on the east, to Pittsburg, Cincinnati, St. Louis, and Chicago on the west; traversing the States of New Jersey, Pennsylvania, Delaware, Maryland, District of Columbia, Virginia, West Virginia, Ohio, Indiana, and Illinois, and the system embraces over 2,000 miles of first-class steel track railway, nearly one-half of its total mileage east of the Ohio River being double-tracked. Its passenger equipment throughout, both in respect to motive power and cars, is of the highest grade.

The main trunk line, East and West, passes through the most picturesque portions of the middle East, and by localities whose very names suggest a flood of historic memories. The Potomac River, which for a time divided the North and South, is first encountered; then comes Frederick, where the battle of Monocacy was fought, and later on Harper's Ferry, where John Brown earned his place in song and story and two of Stonewall Jackson's most famous marches ended. Near by is

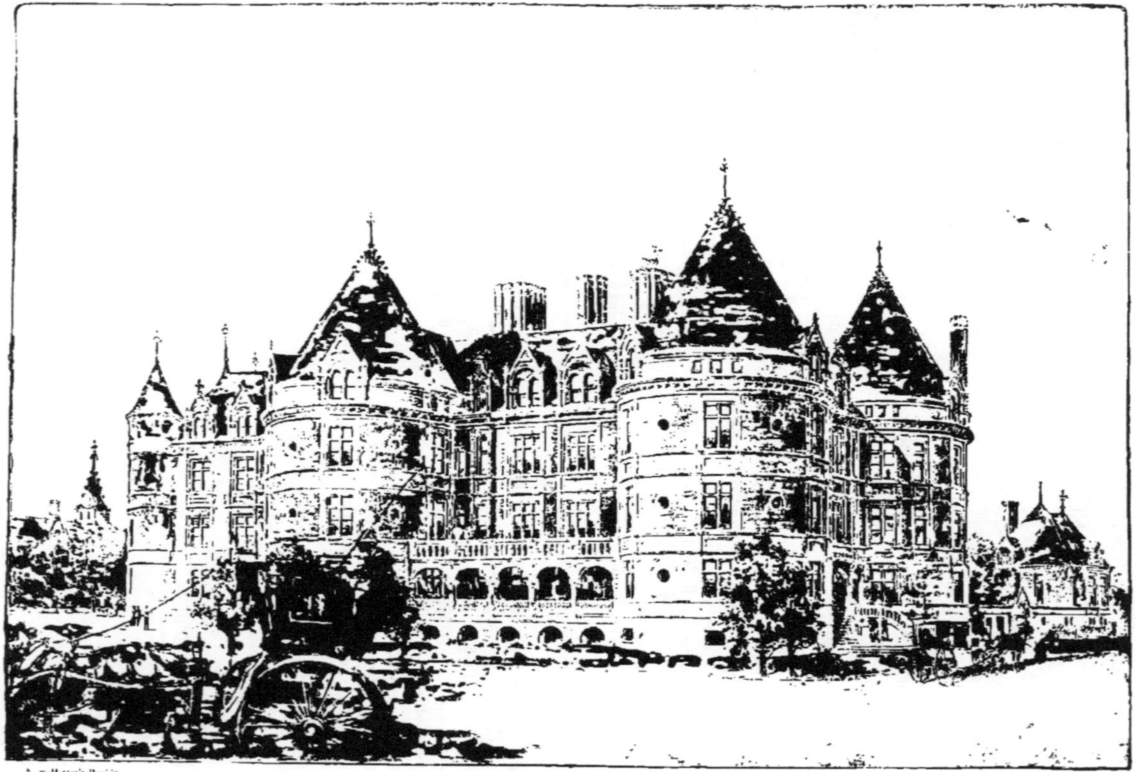

From Harper's Weekly.

Sharpsburg, the scene of the battle of Antietam. Of the scenery surrounding Harper's Ferry no praise need be said, for its charms have been told and pictured the world over, as have those of Shenandoah Valley, which here begins, or, if you please, ends. A little further on the Valley of the Virginia, famous for its many healing springs and scenic charms, opens. Less than seventy miles from the main line are the stupendous and gorgeous Luray caverns.

Continuing on the main line, Martinsburg renews again the war-time recollections, but these are soon driven back to their dusty nooks by the sensations of admiration awakened by the beauty of the scene. Mountains, woods and stretches of river, each unique in its loveliness, are the pictures that chase each other over the retina. At Cumberland the line divides, one branch extending through the Youghiogheny and Monongahela Valleys to Pittsburg and the coal regions, the other over the Alleghenies through the Glades by Deer Park, the famous resort where our Presidents are wont to go holiday-making, and on to Grafton, thence where the line forks again, one branch crossing the Ohio at Parkersburg and proceeding through Cincinnati to St. Louis, and the other crossing the Ohio near Wheeling, passing through Bellaire, Cambridge, Zanesville, Newark, and Mansfield to Chicago.

The grandest scenery on the whole line is seen during the ascent and descent of the Alleghenies. Here is what one writer has to say about it: "At Piedmont commences the seventeen-mile grade, as railroad men call it, and it is one stretch of grandeur that is perhaps without an equal. The locomotive at once gives evidence of the strain to which it is subjected in conquering the steadily increasing altitude, and its hoarse breathings are echoed in the recesses of the distant mountains, where they die away in the still atmosphere, that reverberates its sighful response. The Potomac, dwindling into comparatively insignificant proportions, loses itself at last in the hidden springs of its source. The good-by to the familiar thread of water is with regret; but for this the fury of Savage River, which plunges onward between the gorges of the peak from which it derives its name, abundantly compensates. Deeper now and more sonorous the engine growls as it grasps the steel-clad steps in its steep ascent, and more distant the river that runs in its rocky channel far below. There is a turn in the mountain side, and the steam-choked motor is allowed a few moments' respite. Meanwhile, the eye of the traveler is delighted with what would seem to be an infinity of space were its width not limited by the walls of the gorge, upon the rugged edges of which are to be found, growing in scant soil, the spruce and the pine. Struggling waters trickle down the crumbling sandstone, and vegetation of a sparse description hangs over on the verge of despair. Openings here, great rents in the rocks there, and century-battered peaks that reach appealingly to the clouds, as if in agony at the ruthlessness of the elements which they send down upon them. In short, the entire picture is one continuous testimony to the complete ruin that has been effected by volcanic action. Back around the curve once more, so abrupt and so rocky is the path ahead that one involuntarily pays silent tribute to the hardy men who crushed the mountains and took from their very breasts the substance which now constitutes so solid a base for the train."

No other road in the Eastern States offers to its patrons more pictures than can be seen from the car windows of the Baltimore and Ohio on the way to Chicago. This road has always had a considerable share of the traffic to the Western metropolis, and is now reaching after a greater proportion. One obstacle in its way heretofore has been the difficulty experienced in securing proper terminals in Chicago. This has now been overcome.

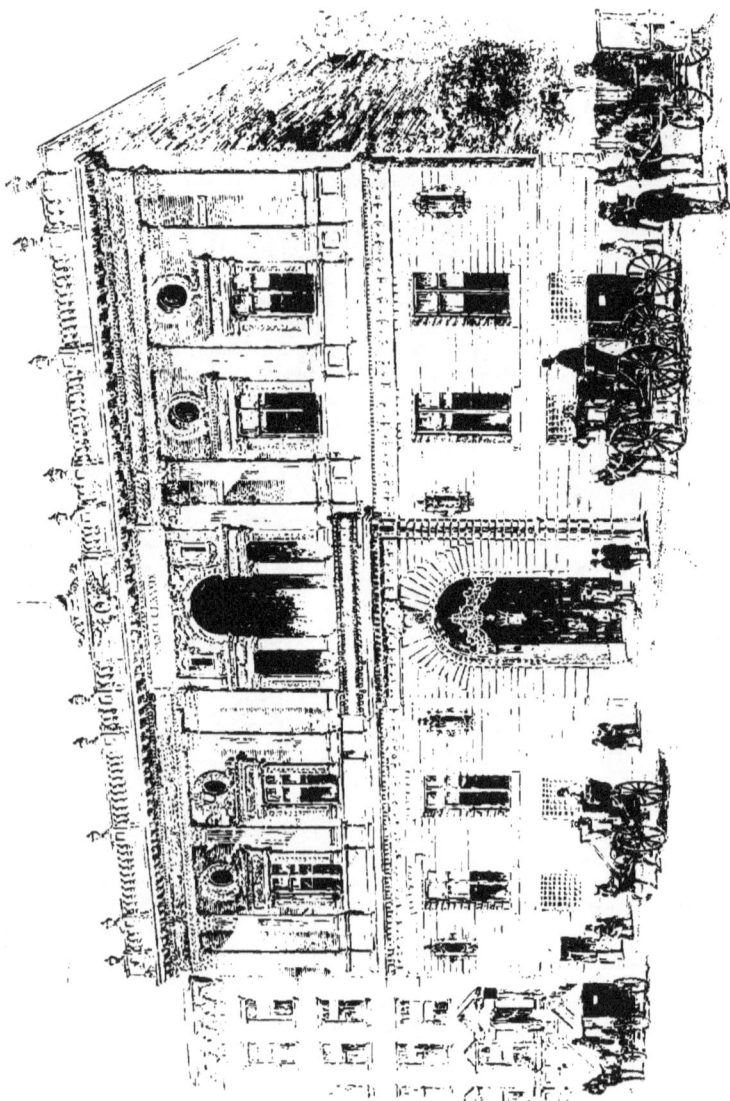

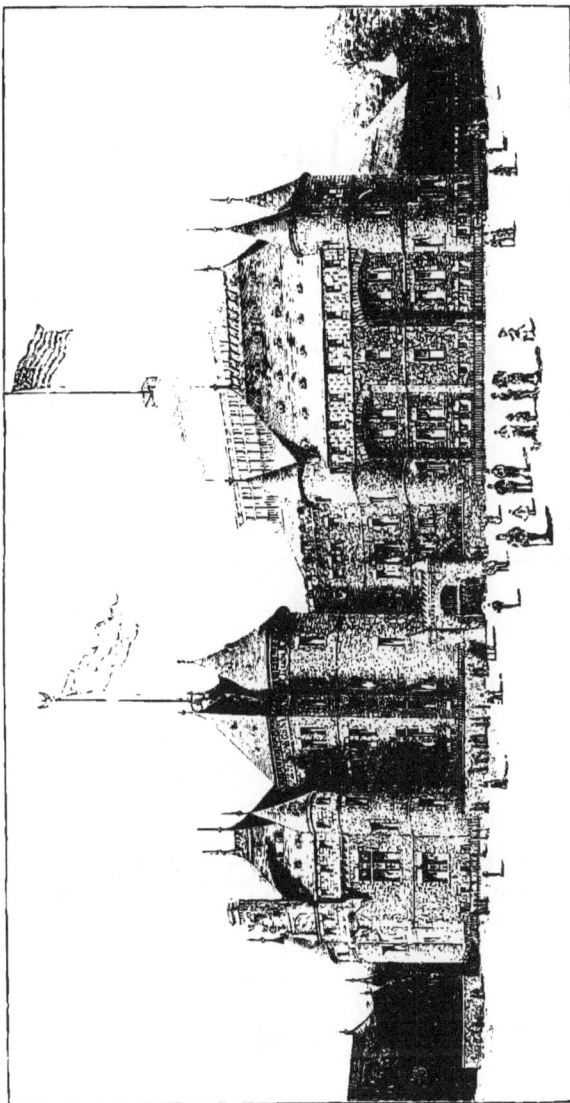

TWENTY-SECOND REGIMENT N. G. S. N. Y. ARMORY.

Boulevard and Sixty-eighth Street, New York.

INTERNATIONAL NAVIGATION CO.

NDER the Ocean Mail Subsidy Act of March 3d, 1891, the two British steamships, "City of New York" and "City of Paris," were granted American registration by a special Act of Congress. Not only do these ships mark a new era in our Merchant Marine, from which protection was withdrawn during the period from 1850 to the present time, but every true-hearted and patriotic citizen of the United States should feel proud that these ships, which can readily and economically be converted into auxiliary naval cruisers, are the finest and fastest steamships in the world.

With the Postal Subsidy Act as a basis, the International Navigation Company of Philadelphia succeeded in getting Congress to pass a bill admitting to American registry foreign built Ocean steamships of over 8,000 tons register capable of a speed of twenty knots and 90% of which were owned by American capital, provided tonnage equivalent in amount to the ships admitted to American registry was contracted for with American shipyards. Not only will the International Navigation Company carry out their contract literally, that is, for tonnage equivalent to the S. S. "New York" and S. S. "Paris," which is 21,000 tons, but with the sound determination which has characterized this company since its inception, American shipyards will receive contracts for the construction of five new steamships of the highest order known to naval architecture, amounting to 55,000 tons, and when this entire fleet is afloat the International Navigation Company will own, operate, and control an aggregate of over 150,000 tons. It is readily appreciated that these two ships, with their five promised sisters the largest, finest, and fastest in the world, are a valuable acquisition to the United States Navy.

To describe the "New York" and "Paris" briefly: they are 580 feet long, 63½ feet wide, and 59½ feet deep; designed and subdivided with water-tight bulkheads to the upper deck, with no openings through them, making the ships absolutely unsinkable. Hydraulic power is employed instead of steam for the daily work of the ships. This machinery is almost absolutely noiseless. The accommodations provided for passengers are constructed with a view to comfort and convenience, and the suites, staterooms, etc., are most luxuriously furnished. The most careful attention has been given to ventilation and sanitary arrangements, which have been scientifically planned.

Southampton, the new terminal of the American Line, is particularly well adapted as a port of entry, as the authorities there, in order to induce the International Navigation Company to make it their foreign home, have expended a large sum of money in creating the proper facilities, and it is expected that at least an half day will be saved in the passage across the Atlantic. Owing to its geographical situation, with connection by land and water with all parts of the world, it is very

MANHATTAN ELEVATED RAILWAY—FORTY-SECOND STREET AND SIXTH AVENUE STATION.

advantageous for passengers as well as for freight shipments. The Company have arranged for special train service, and trains will be in waiting alongside the ship when she arrives at Empress Dock to convey passengers to London, distant only a short hour and a half. The traveler passes through some of the most picturesque parts of Great Britain.

The ceremonies of formally raising the American flag on the "New York" were appropriately performed on Washington's Birthday by President Harrison, in the presence of some of the members of his cabinet and a large gathering of distinguished and representative United States citizens, who were invited by the International Navigation Company to witness this most interesting ceremony. An elaborate programme was arranged for the day. The steamer left her berth on the North River and steamed to a point opposite the Battery, where she anchored and waited for the two special trains which conveyed the guests from Washington and Philadelphia. At noon the special tenders arrived alongside and, amid the roar of cannon from the U. S. S. "Chicago," which was anchored a short distance away, and the music "Hail to The Chief," by the Navy Yard Band, President Harrison boarded the "New York." Under guard of the Naval Reserves, of which there were on board files from the Pennsylvania and New York Battalions, the President was escorted by Mr. Griscom, the President of the Company, to the taffrail, where, after a short speech by Congressman Bourke Cockran, who was the mover of the bill naturalizing the ship, and a speech by President Harrison, who concluded as follows: "I deem it an entirely appropriate function that the President of the United States should lift this American flag," the star-spangled banner was raised. Such a scene has never before been witnessed. Through an ingenious arrangement the steamer was instantly dressed with flags from stem to stern, salutes were fired from the "Chicago," the forts in the harbor, and by the cannon of the Navy Yard, and cheer after cheer went up from the thousands of spectators both on board the ship and on the numerous river craft which surrounded the steamer. The piers, bulkheads, and the Battery were crowded with spectators. After the ceremonies had taken place, luncheon was served in the magnificent saloon, which was handsomely decorated. It had been arranged that the steamer should convey the guests down the bay and out to sea, but owing to inclement weather that part of the programme was omitted.

The "New York" sailed on her initial trip to Southampton Saturday, February 25th, and was given a grand reception on her arrival there by the municipal authorities, it being considered an event of enormous interest to the city of Southampton; it being the first time a modern trans-atlantic liner had steamed into the Port to make it its foreign home. The flag-raising ceremonies were performed on board the "Paris" Tuesday, March 7th, 1893, and, although of great interest, the ceremonies were private. The Directors of the Company, with their families and a few invited guests, were present. The Company has recently acquired from the City the largest and finest pier in New York Harbor, at the foot of Vesey Street, and known as New Pier 14, or Washington Pier. This they are rapidly fitting up in the most approved manner, and it will probably be made, in many respects, the most commodious pier in the world, in its admirable provision for passengers and freight. The rates of first-cabin passage are from $50 to $650, depending on the ship, the season, the number in a state-room, and the location. When shipping freight to Europe, don't forget the American Line.

COTTON EXCHANGE,

Corner William Street and Exchange Place, New York.

Missouri Pacific Railway.

St. Louis to

Chair Cars Free.
Fast Mail Route.

All Points West.

ALL TRAINS thoroughly
equipped with the Celebrated
Pintsch Gas=Light System.

GEO. C. SMITH, Assistant General Manager.   ST. LOUIS, MO.

H. C. TOWNSEND, General Passenger and Ticket Agent.   ST. LOUIS, MO.

W. E. HOYT, General Eastern Passenger Agent,   391 Broadway, NEW YORK.

88

Eagle Standard Pencils.

EAGLE DRAUGHTING PENCILS,

No. 314.

Contains a Deep Black Lead.
Smoothest Pencil Made.

EAGLE STEEL PENS.

Made entirely in New York by a New,
Original, and Improved Method. Ask
your stationer for Eagle and accept
no others.

EAGLE PENCIL COMPANY,

73 FRANKLIN STREET,
NEW YORK.

ALBERT AUGUSTUS POPE.

ALBERT AUGUSTUS POPE, the founder of the bicycle industries in the United States, was born in Boston, Mass., May 20th 1843. He traces his genealogy through many well-known New England families of Pope, Pierce, Cole, Stubbs, Neale, and others. His father, Charles Pope, was an active and stirring business man; and his mother, a daughter of Capt. James Bogman, of Boston, was a lady of rare discernment and quiet decision of character, who taught her son the habits of economy, order, and method, to the exercise of which he attributes much of his success in life. When young Pope was only nine years of age, his father met with business reverses which placed the family in decidedly straightened circumstances. Albert began at once his life of work and business activity by riding a horse to plow for a neighboring farmer in Brookline, which was his home at that time. Three years later he commenced buying fruit and vegetables off the farmers and selling them to the neighbors, showing his innate ability as a manager by employing boys to assist him and reaping a profit from their labors. He soon had between forty and fifty customers, and in one season this business yielded him a profit of one hundred dollars. During this time he received a fair public-school education, which was all the training he ever had from schools, though by careful reading and persistent application he has obtained an exceptional fund of general knowledge. At the age of fifteen he left the high school and secured employment in the Quincy market, and later on took a position with a firm dealing in shoe findings. While there he did all the work of a porter, carrying heavy bags of pegs and one hundred pound bales of thread-work that would not be imposed on a full-grown man in these days, and for this he received only four dollars a week, two of which he paid for board and saved money out of the balance. An accurate account of his expenses shows that he exercised the strictest economy. The store was five miles from his home, yet he frequently walked to and from business in order to save the car fare of sixteen cents. When the war broke out he began the study of military tactics, joining the Salignac's Zouaves and the Home Guards of Brookline, of which company he soon became captain. So intense was his interest that he kept a musket in the store, and with it drilled his fellow clerks and the "bosses" whenever business would permit. At nineteen years of age he joined the volunteer forces of the Union Army, and went to the front as second lieutenant of the 35th Massachusetts Infantry, August 22, 1862. His promotion to first lieutenant, March 23, 1863, and to captain, April 1, 1864, are evidences of his ability and valor. He was employed upon important detached services, and acted as commander of his regiment on many occasions when the colonel was absent or disabled. He organized within twenty-four hours a provisional regiment of artillery from the convalescent camp at Alexandria, and with this force he advanced to the defence of Washington, assuming command of Fort Slocum and Fort Stevens with forty-seven pieces of artillery. This was a move which called for great ability in managing men, and it was accomplished with such skill that Captain Pope was highly complimented by his superior officers. He served in the principal Virginia campaigns, was with Burnside in Tennessee, with Grant at Vicksburg, and with Sherman at Jackson Mississippi. He commanded Fort Hell before Petersburg, and in the last attack led his regiment into the city, at the age of twenty-one years. He was brevetted major "for gallant conduct at the battles of Fredericksburg, Va.," and lieutenant colonel "for gallant conduct in the battles of Knoxville, Poplar Springs Church and front of Petersburg," March 13, 1865. After the war, Colonel Pope returned quietly to his former employers, but soon went into business for himself, in slipper decorations and shoe manufacturers' supplies. In 1877 he became enthusiastic over the bicycle, and with his rare foresight, determined to go into their manufacture. This was done under the name of the Pope Manufacturing Company, a corporation for which he furnished the capital and of which he became, and has ever since continued, the President and active Manager. This Company was organized for the making and selling of small patented articles; but within a year Col. Pope had resolved to stake all its future on the bicycle, and he thus made his Company the pioneer in the business. There was not only no demand for wheels at that time, but in many places the prejudice against them was both outspoken and intolerant. This opposition had to be overcome and a market created. Col. Pope exercised great diplomacy in treating this phase of the business. He imported the best cycling literature to be had, bound it up with the advertisement of rival firms and distributed it freely throughout the country. Through the influence and encouragement of the Pope Mfg. Co., home talent also was brought to bear on the question resulting in the production of Mr. Pratt's book, "The American Bicycler," and the founding of the illustrated magazine, "The Wheelman," which cost upwards of $800,000, and which is flourishing as the "Outing" of to-day. The educating process was followed by the opening of the highways and parks for the use of wheelmen, the Company expending thousands of dollars in settling the Central Park case in New York, the South Park matter in Chicago, and the Fairmount Park contest in Philadelphia. The successful organizing and prosperous growth of this industry bear a well deserved tribute to Col. Pope as a promoter and manager of large business interests and as a financier of strength and fertility. Col. Pope is a director in many banking and business corporations and his advice is sought after and valued.

For some years he has been pioneer in the great movement for highway improvement and has contributed liberally of his means and time for the advancement of this project. His speeches on this subject have been widely read and quoted. His latest move for a comprehensive road exhibit at the Columbian Exposition has aroused the press and the public in general to the importance of the road question.

He married Sept. 20, 1871, Abbie, daughter of George and Matilda (Smallwood) Linder, of Newton, Mass., and they have four sons and one daughter.

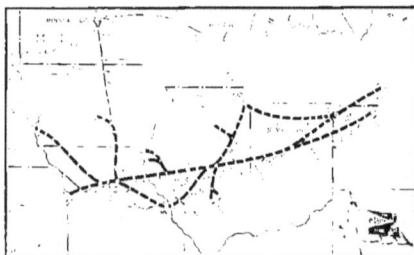

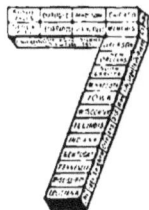

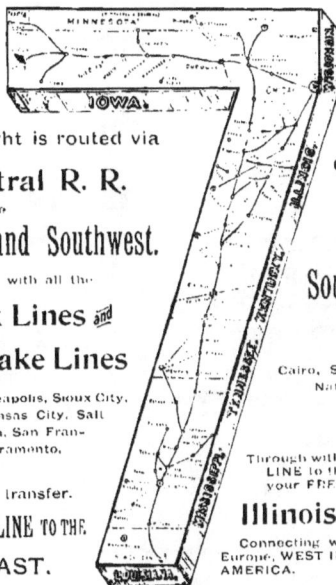

THE NEW MILLION DOLLAR PASS-
ENGER STATION of the Illinois Central
Railroad at 12th Street, Chicago, which
will be completed before the time of the opening
of the World's Fair, will be one of Chicago's
great buildings, in whose architectural beauty,
adaptation to modern requirements, there will
be reason to be justly proud. The natural
beauty and charm of its location is probably
unsurpassed among railroad stations in the
country. On the east and north it overlooks
the sparkling waters of Lake Michigan, in summer time teeming with commercial life and ani-
mation, and from off its surface cooling breezes
are wait to cool the heat waves emanating from
a great city. Facing the front of the Station

**The
Illinois Central
Railroad
and the
World's Fair.**

is the Lake Front Park, while its direct approach is from Chicago's famous Michigan Avenue, a
boulevard typical of the wealth and fashion of this most marvelous City, all blending in graceful
harmony.

Showing entrance
to the City of Chicago over its
elevated tracks direct to, and in full view of,
the grounds and buildings of the World's Columbian Exposition.

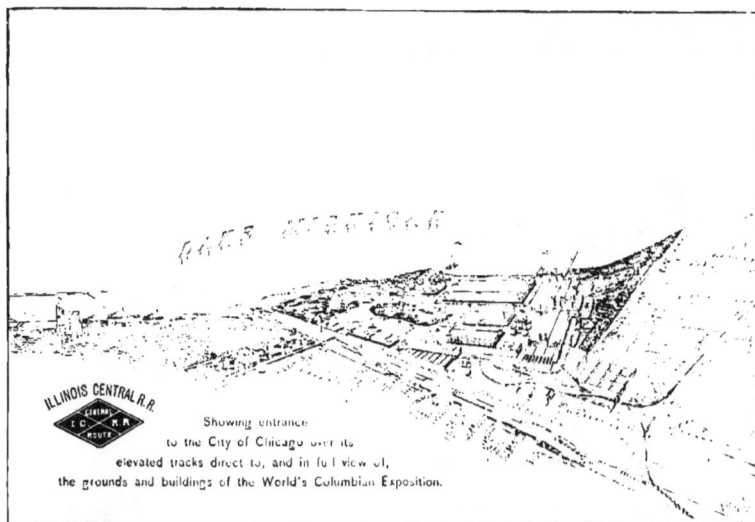

The
Illinois Central
Railroad
and the
World's Fair.

AS will be seen by the illustration above, the tracks of the Illinois Central at Chicago run directly to the World's Fair entrance, in consequence of which that Road will necessarily be the principal means of getting from the City proper to the Exhibition Grounds in 1893. The suburban service of the "Central" is already favorably known as the largest and most complete of its kind in the country, which is the strongest possible argument that its WORLD'S FAIR SERVICE will be efficient.

For the proper handling of the enormous traffic which the Illinois Central Railroad will be called upon to perform, most extensive preparations are now under way, including the purchase of three hundred special cars, to be used exclusively in the World's Fair service, and the traffic in and out of Chicago will be carried on an eight-track roadbed, elevated for over two miles.

Its facilities for suburban, World's Fair, through passenger and freight trains, are independent of the other. It will also be noted that all through and local trains in their departure and arrival through Chicago city limits pass the World's Fair Buildings and surroundings, of which, on account of the elevation of the tracks, a most extensive view is obtained from the car windows. This latter feature is peculiar to the Illinois Central Railroad, for it is the only Road entering and leaving Chicago in FULL VIEW OF THE WORLD'S FAIR GROUNDS AND BUILDINGS.

SOUTHERN PACIFIC COMPANY.

"SUNSET ROUTE."

Morgan's Louisiana & Texas R.R. & S.S. Co., Houston & Texas Central Railway, Mexican International R.R.

TRI-WEEKLY LINE

Sailing from Pier 25, North River, foot of North Moore St., New York, every Tuesday, Thursday and Saturday, at 3 P. M.

IRON STEAMERS

ALGIERS,	EXCELSIOR,	CHALMETTE,	MORGAN CITY,
EL PASO,	NEW YORK,	EL MONTE,	EL DORADO,
EL MAR,	EL SUD,	EL SOL,	EL NORTE,
		EL RIO,	

Taking Freight for

MISSISSIPPI RIVER POINTS,

And all Points in

LOUISIANA,	COLORADO,	ARIZONA,
MISSISSIPPI,	NEW MEXICO,	CALIFORNIA, and
TEXAS,	OLD MEXICO,	CENTRAL AMERICA.

MARK: MORGAN'S LINE SHIP AT PIER 25, N. R.

For Shipments originating at Points other than New York, Mark and Consign "MORGAN LINE, Care E. Hawley, 343 Broadway, New York." Send for Stencil.

For Through Rates, Bills of L   and   other information, apply to

E. HAWLEY, Assistant General Traffic Manager,
343 Broadway, New York.

B. B. BARBER, Agent,	E. E. CURRIER, N. E. Agent,	R. J. SMITH, Agent,
No. 209 East German St., Baltimore.	No. 192 Washington St., Boston.	44 South 3rd St., Phila.

New York, Susquehanna & Western R. R. Company.

15 CORTLANDT ST., NEW YORK.

New York Freight Depot, Pier 16, North River.
Jersey City Freight Depot, First and Green Streets.

REACHING

HACKENSACK, N. J.	PATERSON, N. J.	PASSAIC, N. J.	BUTLER, N. J.
OGDENSBURGH, N. J.	FRANKLIN (Sussex	HAMBURG, N. J.,	DECKERTOWN, N. J.
MIDDLETOWN, N. Y.	Co.), N. J.	SPARTA, N. J.	BLAIRSTOWN, N. J.
DELAWARE, N. J.	COLUMBIA, N. J.	DEL. WATER GAP, Pa.	STROUDSBURG, Pa.

THROUGH FREIGHT RATES TO POINTS ON

BOSTON & MAINE R. R.   CENTRAL R. R. OF NEW JERSEY.
NEW YORK, ONTARIO & WESTERN R. R.   PENNSYLVANIA R. R.
PHILADELPHIA & READING R. R.   PENNSYLVANIA, POUGHKEEPSIE
& BOSTON R. R.

New York Rates to and from all principal Western Points.

C. D. McKELVEY, General Superintendent.   I. I. DEMAREST, Gen'l Freight Agent.

Jacksonville. St. Augustine & Indian River Railway

"THE ST. AUGUSTINE ROUTE."

From JACKSONVILLE via St. Augustine, Ormond, Daytona, New Smyrna and Titusville to ROCKLEDGE on the INDIAN RIVER.

✳ CONNECTIONS ✳

AT JACKSONVILLE —With S., F. & W. and F. C. & P. Railways and the Clyde Steamship Line.

AT PALATKA   With J., T. & K. W. and Florida Southern Railways, St. Johns River and Ocklawaha River Steamers.

AT ROCKLEDGE —With Steamers for all points on INDIAN RIVER and LAKE WORTH.

W. L. CRAWFORD,   JOSEPH RICHARDSON,
General Superintendent.   General Passenger Agent.

THE NEW YORK, ONTARIO
AND WESTERN RAILWAY.

OF all the railroads leading from New York, none can claim a more beautiful route across the State of New York than can the New York, Ontario & Western Railway. The ferries for this road leave the city at the foot of Jay and West Forty-second Streets, and the trains, after leaving the station at Weehawken, pass through the Weehawken tunnel, and run north just west of the Palisades through the beautiful Hackensack Valley. Near Haverstraw the road tunnels the mountain and emerges on the west bank of the river, and from there follows closely its shores through the Highlands of the Hudson, under the military grounds at West Point, to Cornwall. From Cornwall the route is northwesterly across the State, and the region traversed includes the counties of Orange, Sullivan, Ulster, Delaware, Chenango, Otsego, Madison, Oneida and Oswego, a section abounding in beauty, with its mountain summits rising 3,000 feet above the sea, its narrow, exquisitely-lovely valleys, its numberless trout streams, its gem-like lakes, its rugged hillsides and its quiet nooks. The whole region is free from malarial fevers. The greater part of it is above the level of hay fever and rose-colds, and its comparative dryness and uniformity of temperature, together with the resinous perfume of the pines, hemlocks and cedars, make it a desirable region for persons afflicted with pulmonary diseases. One of Brooklyn's foremost physicians says

"It is the consensus of the opinions of many prominent medical men who have given the 'climatic' treatment of consumptives careful study, that we have on the western slope of the Apalachian system (Sullivan and Delaware counties) climatic conditions throughout the whole year, as good, if not superior to those on the eastern slope of the Cordilleran chain, i. e., in Colorado, New Mexico, Arizona, etc."

In the past few years, this region has grown rapidly in the favor of "city people," and each year, more and more residents of New York and vicinity are sending their families up among the numerous farms, boarding-houses and hotels that dot the hills and valleys of this favored region, to renew their health and strength. These hotels, farms and boarding-houses have been collected by the Company into a pamphlet of 160 pages, beautifully illustrated, called "Summer Homes," and it is distributed free by the Railroad Company upon application to the General Passenger Agent, J. C. Anderson, 56 Beaver Street, New York.

Besides the main line running from New York to Oswego, on Lake Ontario, the Company operate the Ellenville, Delhi, and New Berlin Branches ; the Utica Division, running into Utica and Rome. The most important division is probably that leading from Hancock to Scranton, called the Scranton Division, and running down through the Wyoming Valley to Carbondale and Scranton. From this portion of the road the Company get their famous Lackawanna Valley Coal, which is handled by the Sales Agents, Messrs. Dickson & Eddy, 29 Broadway, N. Y.

With its own line and connections, the O. & W. takes freight from New York to a large majority of the cities and towns of central New York and Eastern Pennsylvania, and it prides itself on its quick time in delivering it. It makes also the lowest rates of passenger fare in connection with its through trains and free reclining chair cars, than any road from New York, and with its fast freight line, the Ontario Despatch makes the lowest all-rail rates to the West. The Officers of the N. Y., O. & W. Ry. are : T. P. Fowler, President; J. B. Kerr, Vice-President; R. D. Rickard, Secretary-Treasurer; J. E. Childs, General Manager; J. C. Anderson, General Freight and Passenger Agent, with General Offices at 56 Beaver St., N. Y.

The UNION PACIFIC SYSTEM.

Mark and consign freight care of

Union Pacific System
at Missouri River.

For rates and all information apply to

GENERAL EASTERN AGENCY,

287 Broadway, New York,

or the following offices:

New England Agency,
290 Washington Street,
Boston, Mass.

and

Ferguson Block,
Pittsburgh, Pa.

The most direct route to

San Francisco,
Sacramento,
Los Angeles,
Portland, Seattle,
Tacoma,
Spokane,
Lincoln,
Fremont,
Hastings,
Grand Island,
Topeka,
Denver,
Colorado Springs,
Pueblo,
Trinidad,
Leadville,
Santa Fe,
Salt Lake,
Ogden, Butte,
Helena,
Anaconda,

and all points in

Kansas,
Nebraska,
Colorado,
Wyoming,
Montana,
Utah, Idaho,
California,
Oregon and
Washington.

105

The Plant System.

Comprising the

Savannah, Florida & Western Railway,

Charleston & Savannah Railway,

Brunswick & Western Railway,

Alabama Midland Railway,

South Florida Railroad,

Silver Springs, Ocala & Gulf R. R.

Plant Steamship Line.

To the Cotton Fields and Fruit Gardens of Georgia and Alabama.

To the Orange Groves and Phosphate Beds of Florida.

For information apply to

J. D. Hashagen, Eastern Agent,   A. P. Lane, Agent,
    261 Broadway, New York.   268 Washington St., Boston, Mass.

J. B. Andrews, Agent,   C. D. Owens, Traffic Manager,
    205 East German St., Baltimore, Md.   Savannah, Ga.

PENNSYLVANIA

RAILROAD. ———

THE GREAT TRUNK LINE BETWEEN THE # East AND THE West.

THIS LINE, WITH ITS CONNECTIONS, FORMS THE

SHORTEST AND MOST DIRECT ROUTE

BETWEEN THE ATLANTIC SEABOARD AND ALL PORTIONS
OF THE WEST, NORTHWEST, AND SOUTHWEST.

FREIGHT AGENCIES.———

Have been established in all the principal cities, at which arrangements
can be made for the movement of freight to all the principal points in the
territory reached by this line.

Facilities are offered for the transportation of Live Stock, and good accommodations, with
usual privileges, for persons traveling in charge thereof. Shippers intrusting the transportation of their freights to this company can rely with confidence on its speedy transit.

THE RATES OF FREIGHT.———

To any point in the East or West by the Pennsylvania Road are at all times
as Favorable as are Charged by other Railroad Companies.

Any information desired on the subject of freights will be furnished by any of the following :

J. A. ACKLEY, New England Freight Agent,
    205 Washington Street, Boston.
O. J. GEER, General Agent,
    No. 2 Beaver St., New York.
E. G. DIXON, Division Freight Agent,
    10 South Fourth St., Philadelphia.
W. J. ROSE, Division Freight Agent,
    Harrisburg, Pa.
GEO. T. SMITH, Agent,
    1 Astor House and 433 Broadway, N. Y.

S. L. SEYMOUR, Division Freight Agent,
    Pittsburgh, Pa.
H. W. BROWN, Agent,
    Cincinnati, Ohio.
WM. BORNER, General Western Agent,
    Chicago, Ill.
C. S. FREEBORN, Agent,
    St. Louis, Mo.
R. F. FEIST, Agent,
    No. 70 West St., New York.

WM. H. JOYCE,
General Freight Agent, Philadelphia.

CHAS. A. CHIPLEY,
Ass't Gen. Freight Agent, Philadelphia.

GENERAL FREIGHT OFFICE PENNSYLVANIA RAILROAD CO., 243 S. 4th ST., PHILADELPHIA.

Central Railroad of New Jersey

Just a plain business talk, and just as little poetry and sentiment as possible; that is what follows.

YOU are not an Arab, and you have no particular weakness for tents. But you may have had a very strong longing for them some of these sultry nights, when you have hung out of the narrow window in your "modern flat," like the tongue out of the mouth of a panting dog. The comparison is homely, but so is the unpleasant fact that you get modern improvements in plenty, but little of the old-fashioned, but indispensable, commodity known as fresh air anywhere within the close town. You are crowded, and so are your neighbors, and it makes you more irritable when you get home at night, and not any the less so when you come to the office in the morning. The hours in which you travel between your office and your home, and the indulgence in that delightful method of rapid transit between heaven and earth, suspended by a car strap, is not calculated to add to your good spirits. Still you go on, morning and night, day after day and year after year. Why? Because you must or because you want to struggle for breath that way all your life? Well, hardly. You surely do not live that way of your choice, and you need not so live because you cannot change it.

In less time than it takes to travel between Harlem and your down town office, and at but very little greater cost, if any, you can reach delightful spots where every convenience of the town is introduced without any of its inconveniences; where every breath of air purifies the lungs instead of poisoning them; where bright eyes and rosy cheeks will be the quick response to nature's all-powerful doctoring. And nature submits no doctor's bills after the cure.

The Central Railroad of New Jersey can offer you all this, and will not require you to pass through any of the discomforts of elevated railway travel. Comfortable seats, luxurious, well ventilated passenger coaches, quick time over the finest four-track road-bed in the world, polite employes, frequent trains and trains at almost all hours, make travel between the suburban settlements on the line of this road and your place of business in the metropolis, the beau ideal of comfort and convenience.

There are three divisions of our suburban system, the first ending at Roselle, and including between that and New York, Communipaw, Claremont, Greenville, five stations of Bayonne City, Elizabethport, Elizabeth and E. Mora. The second division extends to Dunellen, and includes Cranford, Westfield, Fanwood, Netherwood, Plainfield, Grant Avenue and Evona. The third division extends as far as Somerville, including Bound Brook and Finderne.

For the clerk, whose duties begin early in the morning, there are accommodations from the various points on the several divisions that will bring him in in the morning as early as 5.00 o'clock. Between that and 8.00 o'clock there are seven trains from points on the third division and between, **You can reach Liberty Street** from extreme points on the second and third divisions in an hour and less.

For the woman of the house, who goes to town to do her shopping or to attend the matinée, there is any number of trains which will bring her into the city, give her an hour or two for shopping, and still ample time to attend the matinée without leaving her home earlier than 11.00, and proportionately later than that, as her home is nearer the city. Leaving any point on the suburban system after 12.30 o'clock in the afternoon, she reaches the city in ample time for the afternoon's pleasure.

For the visitor, who has protracted his stay on the lover, in faithful attendance upon one of the many bright and attractive belles, features of our beautiful suburban settlements, there are trains for the city as late as 11.30 and past midnight. The theatre party can reach town on seven trains between 6.15 and 7.30 p. m., giving them an abundance of time. It will not be necessary for this theatre party to stop in the city, because at 11.30 and 12.15 at night there are trains to convey them to any place on the suburban system. Should they be very belated, there is a train as late as 1.00 o'clock in the morning, going to the extent of the first division.

The painter, who has put the house in presentable shape for the early morning readers of our dailies, can fold away his apron, and seated near his away an hour or two after that or troubled to get before he may take his train home, for at 4.30 a. m. a train leaves the city which will enable him, within less than an hour, to rest his weary limbs in his own bed and amid his home comforts. Between 3.00 and 8.00 o'clock, there are no less than thirty-four trains leaving the city, giving hooker and bricklayer alike their own time to get home. The early morning printers' train runs seven days a week, as does also the 12.15 train. There is, in fact, every reasonable accommodation on Sunday just as well as during the week. There are 142 trains a day during the week, there are 57 on Sunday; and there is probably not a resident of New York to-day, no matter what his occupation or his hours may be, whom the time upon this road would not accommodate. The question then is: Why should you continue to live in quarters where you are crowding others, and where others are crowding you? If you rent along this line you will get better accommodations, and a much more roomy and comfortable dwelling for less money; and, with all its boasted advantages, your flat will not hold a candle to it. Why should you jeopardize the lives of your dear ones where the lack of ventilation is bound to be a source of failing health? Why should you not next some of your holidays, on some bright sunny day take a trip on the **Central Railroad of New Jersey** and convince yourself of the beauty of its suburban settlements, and the coziness and the comforts of suburban home life? Why should you not take advantage of the superior facilities offered along this line for acquiring a home which in the course of time will be your own?

The officers and employes of this Company will always be found ready and willing to impart any information sought, either at the general office in New York, or at any of the stations on their line.

Delaware, Lackawanna & Western Railroad Company.

FAST FREIGHT LINES:

LACKAWANNA LINE.
GREAT EASTERN LINE.
NEW YORK DESPATCH REFRIGERATOR LINE.
NORTH-WEST DESPATCH FAST FREIGHT LINE.
AMERICAN TRANSPORTATION CO.
LACKAWANNA LIVE STOCK EXPRESS.
LACKAWANNA & BOSTON LINE.

LAKE LINES:

LACKAWANNA TRANSPORTATION CO.
LAKE ERIE TRANSPORTATION CO.
CLOVER LEAF LINE.
NORTHERN STEAMSHIP CO.
UNION TRANSIT CO.

B. A. HEGEMAN, Traffic Manager,   HENRY C. HICKS, Ass't Gen'l Freight Agent.
26 Exchange Place, New York.

R. S. ROBERTSON, General Eastern Freight Agent,
429 Broadway, New York.

A. FELL, Western Freight Manager, Buffalo, N. Y.

Reading Railroad System

Philadelphia and Reading R.R.,
Lehigh Valley R.R.

Between New York and Philadelphia,
The Anthracite and Bituminous Coal Fields.

Northern, Central and Western New York,
and Fast Freight Lines to the West,
North and South-west.

Modern Equipment. Refrigerator, and Eastman Summer and
Winter Fruit Cars.

Fast Freight Lines operating over the Reading System from New York.

Traders Despatch,
Lehigh and Wabash Despatch,
Lake Shore Lehigh Valley Route,
Lehigh Valley Despatch,
Lehigh Valley Transportation Co.,
Northern Steamship Co., } Rail and Lake Lines,
Diamond Despatch Canal and Lake Lines.

General Eastern Freight Office, 235 Broadway.

T. J. KLASE,
Gen. Eastern Freight Agent.

JOHN TAYLOR.
Gen. Traffic Manager.
Philadelphia, Pa.

B. H. BAIL,
Gen. Freight Agent,
Philadelphia, Pa.

ERIE LINES

New York, Lake Erie & Western Railroad,
New York, Pennsylvania & Ohio Railroad,
Chicago & Erie Railroad.

Fast Freight Lines.

QUICK TIME BETWEEN NEW YORK AND ALL POINTS EAST, AND THE WESTERN, NORTHWESTERN AND SOUTHWESTERN STATES AND THE CANADAS.

ERIE DESPATCH:
F. D. HUNTER, Acting General Manager, New York.

COMMERCIAL EXPRESS FAST FREIGHT LINE:
J. A. MOORE, General Manager, Buffalo, N. Y.

INTERSTATE DESPATCH:
H. C. DIEHL, Manager, Buffalo, N. Y.

UNION DESPATCH—Lake and Rail, during season of navigation.
WASHINGTON BULLARD, General Manager, Buffalo, N. Y.

QUICK TIME, THROUGH CARS, LOW RATES.

Principal Agencies: New York, Rochester, Boston, Philadelphia, Newark, N. J., Albany, Cleveland, Cincinnati, Columbus, Dayton, O., Urbana, O., Salamanca, Toledo, O., Indianapolis, Evansville, Ind., Peoria, Ill., Minneapolis, Chicago, St. Paul, St. Louis, Kansas City, Leavenworth, Louisville, Omaha, Council Bluffs.

S. P. SHANE, General Freight Agent, N. Y., P. & O. R. R., Cleveland, O.
C. L. THOMAS, Asst. General Freight Agent, C. & E. R. R., Chicago, Ill.
J. DEUEL, Asst. General Freight Agent, N. Y., L. E. & W. R. R., New York.

GEORGE G. COCHRAN,
Traffic Manager, NEW YORK.

H. B. CHAMBERLAIN,
Gen. Freight Agent, NEW YORK.

GENERAL OFFICES: 21 Cortlandt St., New York City.
WESTWARD FREIGHT OFFICES: 401 Broadway, New York City.
WESTERN OFFICE: Phoenix Building, Chicago, Ill.

iii

GRAND TRUNK

AND THE

CHICAGO & GRAND TRUNK RY'S

FORM THE GREAT THROUGH LINE

BETWEEN THE

EAST AND THE WEST,

THROUGH THE

ST. CLAIR TUNNEL,

"The Link that Binds Two Great Nations."

For rates to points in Canada and the United States, and other information, apply to

J. BURTON,	O. S. COCKEY,
General Freight Agent, MONTREAL.	General Agent, 291 Broadway, NEW YORK.
J. W. PETERS, Agent,	F. A. HOWE, Agent,
260 Washington St., BOSTON, MASS.	Home Insurance Bldg., CHICAGO, ILL.

L. J. SEARGEANT, GENERAL MANAGER,

MONTREAL, P. Q.

112

☀ SANTA · Fé · SYSTEM ☀

❀

ATCHISON, TOPEKA & SANTA FÉ
RAILROAD COMPANY.

St. Louis & San Francisco Railway.
Gulf, Colorado & Santa Fé Railway.
Atlantic & Pacific Railroad.
Colorado Midland Railway.
Southern California Railway.
Sonora Railway.

Mark and consign your freight
care

SANTA FÉ LINE,
Chicago,
or

FRISCO LINE,
St. Louis.

For rates of freight, bills of lading, and all information, apply to

261 BROADWAY, NEW YORK.
29 SOUTH 6th ST., PHILADELPHIA.
332 WASHINGTON ST., BOSTON.
98 EXCHANGE ST., BUFFALO.
303 BANK OF COMMERCE B'LD'G, PITTSBURGH.
169 WALNUT ST., CINCINNATI.
213 BANK ST., CLEVELAND.
63 GRISWOLD ST., DETROIT.
212 CLARK ST., CHICAGO.
101 NORTH B'WAY, ST. LOUIS.

❀

☀ SANTA · Fé · SYSTEM ☀

DENVER & RIO GRANDE RAILROAD

To the Traveling Public!

IN SELECTING YOUR ROUTE ACROSS THE CONTINENT
BEAR IN MIND THE FACT THAT THIS IS THE

· · · · ONLY LINE

BETWEEN

DENVER, SALT LAKE CITY
AND OGDEN

OFFERING
PASSENGERS

Choice of Two Routes

WITH THROUGH
PULLMAN PALACE BUFFET AND
TOURIST SLEEPING CARS
BETWEEN

Denver, San Francisco
and Los Angeles.

The New Standard Gauge Line leaves the old one at Salida and passes through Leadville and Glenwood Springs, forming a junction with the old line, via Marshall Pass and Black Canyon, at Grand Junction.
The old line will be operated as before, and trains run in connection, ALL CLASSES OF TICKETS being optional.
This change of line does not lessen our claim to the title of the "SCENIC LINE OF THE WORLD," as the new line is replete with scenic attractions not equalled by any line across the Continent.

MAPS, PAPERS, ETC., Containing descriptive and statistical information, will be furnished free on application, either in person or by mail, to any of the following agents of this Company.

S. K. HOOPER, General Passenger and Ticket Agent. 318 Equitable Building, Denver, Colo.

F. A. WADLEIGH, Ass't Gen. Pass. & Ticket Agent, Denver, Colo.

T. W. BECKER, General Agent, 379 Broadway, New York.

J. W. SLOSSON, General Agent, 256 Clark Street, Chicago, Ill.

W. F. TIBBITS, Traveling Passenger Agent, Denver, Colo.

W. M. RANK, General Agent Pacific Coast, 219 Front Street, San Francisco, Cal.

H. V. LUYSTER, Traveling Passenger Agent, 1008 Broadway, Kansas City, Mo.

W. R. PECK, City Passenger Agent, Denver, Colo.

ALEXANDER JACKSON, Gen. Agent. Pass. Dept., Pueblo, Colo.

A. McFARLAND, City Ticket Agent. 1662 Larimer St., Denver, Colo.

S. M. BROWN, Joint Agent, Leadville, Colo.

J. M. ELLISON, General Agent, Colorado Springs, Colo.

W. J. SHOTWELL, General Agent, Salt Lake City, Utah.

ELMER CLARK, Contracting Agent, 256 Clark St., Chicago, Ill.

JOSEPH S. REYNOLDS, Contracting Ag't, 256 Clark St., Chicago, Ill.

C. S. ORCUTT, Contracting Agent, 219 Front St., San Francisco, Cal.

C. B. SMITH, Traveling Freight and Pass. Agent, Leadville, Colo.

J. S. GARD, Traveling Freight and Pass. Agent, Salt Lake City.

J. H. WATERS, Joint Agent, Aspen.

H. E. TUPPER, Traveling Passenger Agent, 379 Broadway, New York.

For advice concerning the Denver & Rio Grande Express, which is operated in connection with this Railroad, apply to

C. W. KRAMER, Manager of Express, Equitable Building, Denver, Colo.

115

NORTHERN PACIFIC R.R.

THE

YELLOWSTONE PARK ROUTE

TO MONTANA AND

PACIFIC · COAST.

THROUGH

VESTIBULED ∗ PULLMAN ∗ SLEEPERS

FROM CHICAGO DAILY.

2 ✚ CHOICE OF TWO ROUTES ✚ 2

WISCONSIN CENTRAL or CHICAGO, MILWAUKEE & ST. PAUL RY. and NORTHERN
PACIFIC R. R., to all Points West, including LIVINGSTON,
HELENA, BUTTE, SPOKANE,

TACOMA, SEATTLE AND PORTLAND.

J. M. HANKAFORD.	CHAS. S. FEE,	CHAS. B. LAMBORN.	P. B. GROAT,
General Traffic Manager.	Gen'l Pass. and Ticket Ag't.	Land Commissioner.	General Emigration Agent,
ST. PAUL, MINN.		ST. PAUL, MINN.	

W. N. MEARS, Traveling Passenger Agent, 309 Broadway, New York,
GEO. R. FITCH, General Eastern Agent, 309 Broadway, New York.

116

Ⓜⓘ⓭land 🐉 Railway
OF ENGLAND.

EXPRESS TRAINS BETWEEN

LIVERPOOL (Central)

AND **LONDON** (St. Pancras)

AT CONVENIENT INTERVALS.

THE MIDLAND is the only line between Liverpool and London passing through the Magnificent and Picturesque Scenery of the

PEAK OF DERBYSHIRE

AND THE VALE OF MATLOCK.

SPECIAL EXPRESS TRAINS run from · · · · · ·

LIVERPOOL (CENTRAL) TO LONDON (ST. PANCRAS)

For a reasonable number of Passengers, when required in connection with steamers from America.

Holders of First-Class Tickets,
Via The Midland Railway, can use the **DRAWING-ROOM SALOONS** · · · ·
By the Day Express Trains between Liverpool and London **without extra charge**.

Private Drawing-Room Saloons, with Lavatory and other conveniences, provided for the exclusive use of parties of seven or more, without extra charge.

· · EXPRESS TRAIN SERVICES BETWEEN · ·

LIVERPOOL (EXCHANGE) and SCOTLAND,
· ALSO BETWEEN · ·

LONDON (ST. PANCRAS) and SCOTLAND,

The Direct Route to GLASGOW and GREENOCK (for the Western Highlands and Islands), through the LAND OF BURNS.
EDINBURGH, through MELROSE and the WAVERLEY District.
PERTH, ABERDEEN, INVERNESS, etc., over the FORTH BRIDGE.

BAGGAGE IS CHECKED THROUGH from New York or the Landing Stage at Liverpool to any Hotel, Private Residence, or Railway Station in London.

THE "ADELPHI" HOTEL, LIVERPOOL
(ADELPHI HOTEL COMPANY),
Reorganized, Refurnished, and Redecorated, is now one of the Best of European Hotels.

THE MIDLAND GRAND HOTEL,
Attached to the LONDON (St. Pancras) STATION, is one of the Largest and Best Appointed in Europe.

TICKETS, TIME TABLES, and all information required by travelers may be obtained from the Company's American Agents, Mr. Hurley and Messrs. Thos. Cook & Son, 261 and 262 Broadway, New York; or of Mr. John B. Curtis, Liverpool Agent of

The Midland Railway Company, England.

DERBY.

GEORGE H. TURNER, General Manager.

117

F. A. RINGLER & CO.,

MANUFACTURERS OF

PLATES FOR ALL PRINTING PURPOSES BY VARIOUS PROCESSES,

21 & 23 Barclay St., & 26 and 28 Park Place, New York.

THE NICARAGUA CANAL.

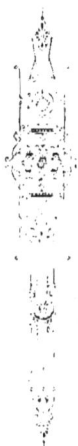

THE

GATEWAY

TO THE

PACIFIC.

THE NICARAGUA CANAL
        CONSTRUCTION COMPANY.

44 Wall Street,

Warner Miller,
    President.

New York.

Colt's Pat. Fire Arms Mfg. Co.

HARTFORD, CONN., U. S. A.

Revolvers,
Rifles,
Shot=Guns.

The 22 Calibre " Lightning " Rifle.

The Double-Barrel Hammerless Shot-Gun.

Material and Workmanship of the Very Best.

HAKE'S Chamois Finish PAPER

Manufactured in all Fashionable sizes,
and Four Tints for Ladies Correspondence.

FOR SALE BY ALL LEADING STATIONERS.

Trade Supplied by Makers.

PH. HAKE MANUFACTURING CO.

NEW YORK, U. S. A.

Display W
Section F

1850. ✵ 1893.

The United States

Life Insurance Co.

In the City of New York.

OFFICERS.

GEORGE H. BURFORD	PRESIDENT.
C. P. FRALEIGH.	SECRETARY.
A. WHEELWRIGHT.	ASSISTANT SECRETARY.
WM. T. STANDEN.	ACTUARY.
ARTHUR C. PERRY.	CASHIER.
JOHN P. MUNN.	MEDICAL DIRECTOR.

FINANCE COMMITTEE.

GEO. G. WILLIAMS.	Prest. Chem. Nat. Bank.
JULIUS CATLIN.	Dry Goods.
JOHN J. TUCKER.	Builder.
E. H. PERKINS, JR.	Prest. Importers' and Traders' Nat. Bank.

The two most popular plans of LIFE INSURANCE are the CONTINUABLE TERM POLICY, which gives to the insured the greatest possible amount of indemnity in the event of death, at the lowest possible present cash outlay; and the GUARANTEED INCOME POLICY, which embraces every valuable feature of investment insurance, and which in the event of adversity overtaking the insured may be used as COLLATERAL SECURITY FOR A LOAN, to the extent of the full legal reserve value thereof, in accordance with the terms and conditions of these policies.

Good Agents, desiring to represent the Company, are invited to address J. S. Gaffney, Superintendent of Agencies, at Home Office.

123

FIFTH AVENUE HOTEL

Madison Square, New York.

The largest, best appointed, and most liberally managed hotel in the city, with the most central and delightful location.

A. B. Darling.

Charles N. Vilas.

E. A. Darling.

Hiram Hitchcock.

Hitchcock, Darling & Co.

FIFTH ✻ AVENUE ✻ HOTEL

Madison Square, New York.

THIS noble pile of white marble, Corinthian architecture, covering eighteen full city lots and accommodating one thousand guests, marks a [...] in the heart of the great City of New York and an era in the history of the Nation's wealth and advancement. It is located at the [...] of the City, upon the charming Madison Square, and at the intersection of the two great streets, Broadway and Fifth Avenue, and convenient to the most important points of interest in the Metropolis.

His Royal Highness the Prince of Wales made the Fifth Avenue his home when in New York in 1860, and its patrons include the names of the most prominent men and women in America—the Presidents, heads [...] of Government Officials, Senators, Congressmen, Judges, Army and Navy Officers, Divines, Physicians, Authors, and in fact all who have attained prominence and celebrity in public and private life, both at home and abroad, and the most distinguished Europeans of rank and title who have visited this country.

It has been the centre of all the great public occasion which the City has witnessed for forty years.

Years have come and gone, new hotels have multiplied with innovations and features introduced to affect and influence patronage, but the Fifth Avenue is as new and fresh as the most recent hotel construction, with [...] and decorated [...] than any of them, and its well-earned reputation as the leading Hotel of the world is more and more assured.

ASPHALT PAVEMENTS

ERE first laid in Paris, France, in 1854. The material used was a lime-stone impregnated with Asphalt, mined in Neuchâtel. Its utility was discovered by the use of the rock upon the road leading from the mine in the nature of Macadam. The use of improved methods and machinery brought it to its present high state.

This class of pavements was soon afterwards adopted by Berlin, London, and other European cities, so that up to the present time (1892) there has been laid 2,033,200 square yards. Berlin heads the list with over one million yards, and Paris following with three hundred and eighty-five thousand yards. Its smoothness, comfort to horse, vehicle and riders, cleanliness, ease of repair and great sanitation led American inventors to adopt, soon after the war, a coal tar substitute. Coal tar pavements were laid in many cities in the United States up to within a few years. They proved failures. A Belgian chemist, experimenting for paving material equal to or superior to the European natural bituminous rock, turned his attention to the large deposit of Asphalt known as the Pitch Lake in the Island of Trinidad. By the combination of this Asphalt with sharp sand, limestone dust and the residuum of petroleum, a pavement superior to those of Europe was made.

The European rock becomes very dense and attains a high state of polish and becomes very slippery, and requires sanding, while the pavement made of Lake Asphalt has a gritty surface, affording a good foothold for horses, besides being more durable.

The Trinidad Lake Asphalt pavement was first laid in this country in quantity on Pennsylvania Avenue in Washington, D. C., in 1876. Its great success there led to its adoption as a standard pavement in over seventy of the largest cities in the United States and Canada, and the present area now covered is upwards of twelve million square yards, making a roadway 26 feet wide 800 miles long, put down by 27 companies and individuals. Of this amount of Trinidad Lake Asphalt Pavement **THE BARBER ASPHALT PAVING COMPANY**, of No. 1 Broadway, New York, has laid, during its fourteen years of existence, over six and one-half million yards.

Information and estimates given upon application.

Cleveland's is the strongest of all pure cream of tartar baking powders, yet its great merit is not its strength, but the fact that it is **pure, wholesome** and **sure.**

" *You're right enough when I tackle you,*" said the little can of Cleveland's baking powder to the big barrel of flour.

(Copyright.)

Instead
Of bread
'Twas lead,
She said,
Till the privilege
was allowed her
To make
And bake
And take
The cake
With Cleveland's
baking powder.

Nº 1

Nº 2

Which is longer ?

To the eye the lower of the above, No. 2, seems to be the longer, but actual measurement proves it to be precisely the same length as No. 1.

To the eye, bread, cake or biscuit made with an Alum or Ammonia baking powder may *look* very nice, but made with

Cleveland's
Baking Powder

it will be finer grained, will keep moist and fresh longer, and will not have a bitter or unpleasant taste; and above all, it will be perfectly wholesome.   *Copyright.*

One rounded teaspoonful of Cleveland's Baking Powder does more and better work than a heaping teaspoonful of any other. A large saving on a year's bakings.

DREXEL & CO.	DREXEL. HARJES & CO.
COR. OF FIFTH AND CHESTNUT STREETS,	11 BOULEVARD HAUSSMANN,
PHILADELPHIA.	PARIS.

DOMESTIC AND FOREIGN BANKERS.

Deposits received subject to Draft. Securities bought and sold on commission. Interest allowed on Deposits; Foreign Exchange, Commercial Credits, Cable Transfers; Circular Letters for Travelers, available in all parts of the world.

ATTORNEYS AND AGENTS OF

MESSRS. J. S. MORGAN & CO., 22 OLD BROAD ST., LONDON.

THE FIRST
NATIONAL
BANK.

BROADWAY AND
WALL STREET,   NEW YORK.

THE

ATIONAL PARK BANK

OF NEW YORK.

)▪◂◂(

Capital, $2,000,000.
Surplus, $3,000,000.

EXTENSIVE SAFETY VAULTS FOR THE CONVENIENCE OF DEPOSITORS
AND INVESTORS. ENTRANCE ONLY THROUGH THE BANK.

131

JEWELL
Belting
Company,

Hartford, Conn.

Manufacturers of

Short Lap,
Pure Oak,
Leather Belting.

GRAND UNION HOTEL.

OPPOSITE
GRAND CENTRAL DEPOT
NEW YORK CITY.

$6.00 ROOMS
$1.00 per day
and Upwards
EUROPEAN PLAN
BAGGAGE
to and from
GRAND
CENTRAL DEPOT
FREE.

PATRONIZED BY TRAVELERS FROM ALL DIRECTIONS

FORD & COMPANY,   PROPRIETORS.

HOTEL MARLBOROUGH.

Covering the entire block on ◎ ◎ ◎
Broadway, between Thirty-sixth
◎ and Thirty-seventh Streets,

◎ ◎ NEW YORK.

LOUIS L. TODD,
Proprietor.

134

SUMMARY

OF THE

29th Annual Statement

OF THE

TRAVELERS

INSURANCE COMPANY,

OF HARTFORD, CONN.

January 1, 1893.

ASSETS ·	$15,029,921.09
LIABILITIES -	12,450,126.85
Surplus to Policy-holders -	$2,579,794.24

LIFE DEPARTMENT

Number Life Policies written to date	71,083
New Life Insurance written in 1892 · · ·	$21,539,732

A gain over 1891 of $5,603,821.

OR OVER 35 PER CENT.

Paid Life Policy-holders to date	$7,755,110
Paid Life Policy-holders in 1892	$845,702

ACCIDENT DEPARTMENT

Number Accident Policies written to date	1,914,807
Number Accident Policies written in 1892	96,605
Number Accident Claims paid in 1892	13,693
Whole number Accident Claims paid	241,281
Amount Accident Claims paid in 1892	$953,116
Whole Amount Accident Claims paid	$14,063,305

Paid Policy-holders in 1892	**$1,798,818**
Total Losses paid since 1864	**$22,718,416**

New York Office, 140 Broadway—R. M. JOHNSON, General Agent.

THE MOST EXTENSIVE MANUFACTURERS IN THE WORLD OF

BILLIARD AND POOL TABLES.

136

The John Good Cordage

AND

Machine Company.

On or about April Tenth will
remove to the Morris Building,
Broad and Beaver Streets

Stewart Building,

New York.

Cordage, Binder Twine,

Machinery.

STATEN ISLAND
TERRA COTTA
LUMBER CO.

Manufacturers of

Salt Glazed Vitrified Sewer and Drain Pipe and Flue Linings, Fire Brick, **Ornamental Front Brick** of all Colors, Architectural Terra Cotta, and **Porous Terra Cotta** or **"TERRA COTTA LUMBER,"** and Hard Tile for Fire-proof Building.

Miners and Shippers of Clay, Fire Mortar, etc.

This Company owns the exclusive right to manufacture Porous Terra Cotta, or "TERRA COTTA LUMBER," in Middlesex Co., N. J., and Richmond Co., N. Y.

FACTORIES: **WOODBRIDGE, NEW JERSEY.**

OFFICES: Equitable Building, **120** BROADWAY, NEW YORK.

EVENING ADDRESS,   Hotel Imperial.

National Cordage Co.

To the Commercial Travelers of America.

Gentlemen: Having been engaged in the business of supplying banks and offices with Desks, Partitions, Counters, etc., for the past twenty-five years, always striving to put the best possible cabinet work on the market, we take pleasure in calling your attention to the record, of which we are proud.

Should you require any Office Furniture, or should you hear of any customers or friends seeking a reliable house for the purpose of securing Office Furniture at the lowest possible price for good work, we ask your active interest and reference in our behalf. We have recently furnished the new and handsome offices of the following firms and corporations: The Central Railroad of New Jersey, The Brooklyn Eagle, Brooklyn Bank, Hide and Leather Bank of New York, Mail and Express, Seabury & Johnson, Germania Fire Insurance Company of New York, American Lithographic Company, Manhattan Storage Company, Cuyler, Morgan & Company, State Trust Company, New York, Brooklyn City Railroad, offices and others.

We are now turning out fixtures and furniture for the Planters' Bank and Trust Company, of Richmond, Va., the Corn Exchange Bank of New York. Harvey, Fiske & Son, The Metropolitan Life Insurance Company, The Connecticut Trust Company, The Charity Organization Society and many others. Our aim is to succeed, and we can guarantee all our work to be first-class. Our stock is the largest in variety of styles, in sizes, and reasonable prices in the world. Our Desks are shipped in large quantities to the European market.

In soliciting the active friendship of the Commercial Travelers of America, it may be added that not a little of our substantial success in business is due to the good will and pride which first-class travelers take in helping American manufacturers who devote themselves to maintain the quality and workmanship of their products.

We shall esteem it a personal favor if you will help our salesmen by notifying them when you hear of any opening for our goods.

Wishing the Commercial Travelers Club of New York good luck, feeling that its future is assured, we remain,   Yours respectfully,

WILLIAM SCHWARZWAELDER & CO.

GERMANIA INSURANCE CO

HIDE AND LEATHER BANK

William Schwarzwaelder & Co.,

Manufacturers of

Bank and Office Furniture,

37 and 39 Fulton Street, New York.

LONG ISLAND LOAN AND TRUST CO

STATE TRUST CO

Established 1760.   *Incorporated 1891.*

P. LORILLARD
COMPANY,

OBACCO,

JERSEY CITY,
NEW JERSEY.

P. Lorillard, Jr., Pres.   *Geo. D. Finlay, V. Pres. and Treas.*

Ethan Allen, Secretary.

Apollinaris

"THE QUEEN OF TABLE WATERS."

"APOLLINARIS is regarded as the leading dietetic Table Water."

NEW YORK TRIBUNE,

"At Banquets, Clubs, and in homes APOLLINARIS Natural Table Water is ever a welcome guest."

N. Y. TIMES.

"The purity of APOLLINARIS offers the best security against the dangers which are common to most of the ordinary drinking waters."

LONDON MEDICAL RECORD.

"APOLLINARIS is exceptionally favored, pure and agreeable. Its value cannot be overestimated in locations where pure drinking water is the exception."

THE MEDICAL RECORD, N. Y.

PIPER-HEIDSIECK

SEC.

Long Famous.
Still Unrivalled.
Intensely Dry.

Pronounced by Connoisseurs a
perfect Champagne.

Sold Everywhere.

THE NIAGARA FALLS POWER COMPANY.

THE NIAGARA FALLS POWER
COMPANY was incorporated by a special
act of the Legislature of the State of New York,
March 31, 1886, for the purpose of constructing,
maintaining, and operating the Hydraulic Tunnel,
and for furnishing power for manufacturing purposes. This Company will be prepared to supply
power about the first of July, 1893.

THE NIAGARA FALLS POWER COMPANY.

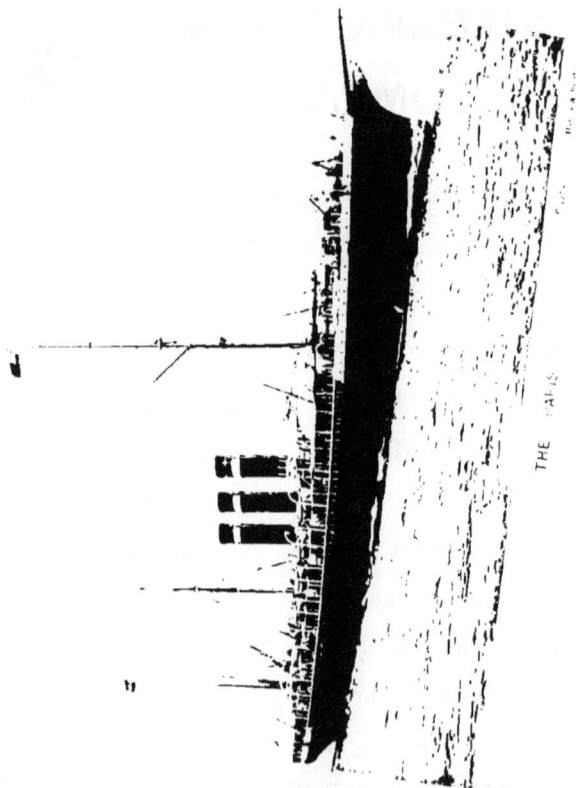

THE PALM

TIME AS QUICK. RATES AS LOW AS
BY ANY RESPONSIBLE COMPETITOR.

MONEY ORDERS

OF THE

ADAMS EXPRESS COMPANY

On sale at its Offices, and payable at nearly every Express Office in the
United States.

Rates:

NOT OVER $5.00, 5 CENTS.

Over $ 5.00, not over $10.00, 8 cents.
"   10.00,   20.00, 10   "
20.00,   "   30.00, 12
30.00,   40.00, 15   "
40.00,   "   50.00, 20   "

148

The AMERICAN EXPRESS... COMPANY.

OFFERING
THE
MOST
PERFECT
FACILITIES
AND
THE
BEST
SERVICE
THROUGHOUT
THE

THE
BUSINESS
MEN'S
SYSTEM.

UNITED STATES.
CANADA AND
EUROPE. . . . .

REHM & CO.

157 Fulton Street, New York City.

Manufacturers, Wholesale and Retail Dealers

Telephone Call. Cortlandt 7○.

AWNINGS AND TENTS.
BUNTING AND SILK FLAGS
AND BANNERS.

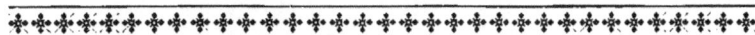

AWNINGS made to order of every description. We also make the Improved Spring Roller Awning.

FLAGS. All kinds and all sizes always in stock ; also made to order for Hotels, Club Houses, Yachts, Steamships, Sailing Vessels, etc.

TENTS. A large assortment always on hand ; also Tents to rent for Fairs, Festivals, Meetings, etc., etc.

The Flags for the Commercial Travelers Club's new building were made by us. A LIBERAL DISCOUNT allowed to all members of the Commercial Travelers Clubs.

Send 6 cents in postage for Catalogue of Awnings and Tents.

Send 6 cents in postage for Catalogue of Flags.

C H LILLEY.

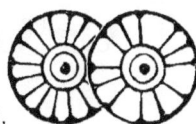

C. G. Gunther's Sons.———

❀

FUR DEALERS
AND FURRIERS

❀

No. 184 Fifth Avenue,
Broadway and 23d Street,
New York.

THURBER, WHYLAND CO.

NEW-YORK.

RELIABLE FOOD PRODUCTS.

THE CAPEWELL HORSE NAILS
Are "The Best in the World" for Horse Owner and Blacksmith.

CITY HEADS.

They are "The best Driving Nail,"

REGULAR HEADS.

THEY NEVER CRIMP in driving in the hardest shoes; they are flexible to set on clinch, and the clinch holds against loosening.

THEY ARE UNIFORM in length, breadth and thickness.

THEY NEVER SPLIT IN DRIVING.

THEY NEVER BREAK UNDER THE HEADS, both of the shoe until it is worn on.

THEY ARE MADE FROM THE BEST SWEDISH IRON RODS, specially imported, the quality of which is unsurpassed in comparison.

CONTROLLED EXCLUSIVELY BY THIS COMPANY.

"The Best Driving Nail."

ANNHEUSER BUSCH BREWING ASSOCIATION.

THE CAPEWELL HORSE NAIL CO., HARTFORD, CONN.

·BINGHAM HOUSE·

MARKET AND

ELEVENTH STS.

Service
and
Appointments
First class
$2.50
per day.

Three Blocks from
Broad St. Station.

PHILADELPHIA.

PA.

· Estate
of
M. Goodin,
A. G. Goodin,
M. H. Goodin,
Proprietors.

Rates :

J. E. KINGSLEY & CO.,

THE CONTINENTAL,

Chestnut Street,
Corner 9th.

PHILADELPHIA, PA.

Unsurpassed by any hotel in location, appointments, organization or Cuisine.

Café and Lunch Counter

IN THE EXCHANGE OF

THE CONTINENTAL.

IT OFFERS TO GENTLEMEN THE CONVENIENCE OF

A SUBSTANTIAL LUNCH, QUICKLY
SERVED, AT REASONABLE PRICES,
IN A SPACIOUS ROOM TASTEFULLY
DECORATED AND DELIGHTFULLY
COOL IN SUMMER. - - - - -

166

THE HEUBLEIN

Hartford, Ct.

AT THE JUNCTION OF

LEWIS, WELLS AND TRUMBULL STREETS,

Facing Bushnell Park.

A Modern Hotel on the European Plan. Hot and Cold Water in every room, also Steam and Open Fire Place. The only Hotel in the United States furnished throughout with imported rugs.

G. F. HEUBLEIN & BRO.,

Proprietors.

THE ✤ POWERS ✤ HOTEL,
ROCHESTER, N. Y.

ABSOLUTELY FIRE-PROOF.

Only First-Class Hotel in the City.

BUCK & SANGER,   -   -   -   PROPRIETORS

THE **Quincy**

AMERICAN
AND EUROPEAN
PLANS.

500 ROOMS.

SINCLAIR & MANN,
BOSTON.

Chas. A. Sinclair.   Geo. G. Mann.

IS one of the best conducted hotels in New England. Noted for its excellence and elaborate appointments, having been refurnished throughout. Strangers, business men, and tourists will find it to their advantage to stop at **The Quincy.** Situated in the very heart of the city, two minutes' walk from Faneuil Hall. Near all principal points of interest. Horse-cars pass the door to depots and all parts of the city. The proprietors pride themselves on the reputation of the cuisine and table, which is the best in New England, everything being served on the most liberal scale.

The Quincy is the only hotel in Boston running its elevator all night. Mail collected and delivered at hotel every hour from 6 A. M. until midnight, a special service having been inaugurated by the proprietors, entirely independent of government delivery, affording quick service for all guests.

The Quincy House Cafe is noted for its English mutton chops, Welsh rarebits, and broiled live lobsters.

The only hotel in Boston running its own carriages. Fare to and from all depots, 25 cents. Intending guests coming to Boston can write or telegraph in advance; carriages will meet them at depots.

New Cafe First-class cuisine and service at reduced prices. Fifteen to thirty per cent. lower than any hotel in Boston. The Quincy will also continue the American Plan, as hitherto. The splendidly appointed Private Dining-Rooms of The Quincy have long been famous for the convenience they afford family gatherings and small parties who desire to be served elegantly, apart from the noise and confusion of a public banquet hall.

Messrs. SINCLAIR & MANN invite the public to inspect the costly and eminently satisfactory system of Fire Escapes just added to the Quincy House, under the supervision and direction of the Inspectors of Buildings for the City of Boston, and officially approved by them February 6, 1893.

This equipment consists of a system of outside iron stairways and balconies passing in front of the windows on every floor, and leading from the roof to the first floor.

A child of five years could reach the ground in safety unaided, and immediate escape is possible for any and every guest without possibility of danger to the person whatever the excitement, peril, or confusion. Seventy-five tons of iron were used in the construction of these stairways and balconies.

The balconies aggregate a total length of nearly a mile.

Twelve thousand dollars represents the cost of this system of fire escapes, which is the largest contract for this purpose ever given by a hotel, and is unparalleled among the hotels of the United States.

The proprietors of The Quincy consider that the comprehensiveness, efficiency, and thoroughness with which these fire escapes have been planned and constructed reflects the highest credit upon Chief Damrell and his assistants.

164

EUGENE MUNSELL
& CO.,
STOVE FOUNDERS,

No. 218 WATER STREET,
NEW YORK.

NORTH CAROLINA,
WYOMING,
AMBER

MICA

HEADQUARTERS MINERS.
WHOLESALE DEALERS.

Phenix Insurance Company,

Brooklyn, N. Y.

Cash Capital, - - -	*$1,000,000 00*
Gross Assets December 31, 1892,	*5,584,704 61*
Liabilities, - - - -	*4,040,960 07*
Surplus as to Policy Holders,	*1,543,744 54*
Losses Paid Since Organization,	*$44,420,594 01*

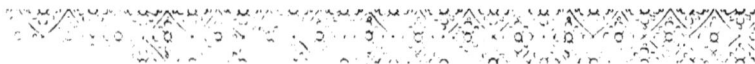

The Liverpool

and London

and Globe

INSURANCE COMPANY,

EMPOWERED AS A STOCK COMPANY.

New York Board,

CHARLES H. MARSHALL, Chairman.
JOHN A. STEWART.
JAMES E. PULSFORD.
JOHN CROSBY BROWN.
EDMUND D. RANDOLPH.

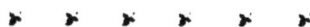

CHIEF OFFICE IN THE UNITED STATES.

45, 47, 49 WILLIAM STREET AND 40, 43 PINE STREET.

NEW YORK CITY

HENRY W. EATON,
Resident Manager.

GEO. W. HOYT,
Deputy Manager.

Statement.

United States Branch

OF THE

Liverpool and London and Globe Insurance Company.

JANUARY 1, 1893.

Assets.		Liabilities.	
Real Estate,	$1,574,500.00	Unearned Premiums,	$3,923,850.30
Loans on Bond and Mortgage,	2,517,547.00	Unadjusted Losses,	575,710.83
U. S. Government Bonds,	1,511,280.00	Perpetual Policy Liability,	337,400.00
City of Boston Bonds,	294,125.00	Miscellaneous,	420,865.00
Cash in Banks,	790,141.85	**Surplus,**	**$3,029,196.76**
Premiums in course of collection,	855,940.22		
Other admitted Assets,	144,349.55		
	$8,193,023.89		$8,193,023.89

Losses.

The amount paid in satisfaction of fire losses in the United States in a period of forty-five years is

$56,241,533.35.

167

46th Annual Statement
of the

Connecticut Mutual
Life Insurance Co.

Of Hartford, Conn.

Net Assets, Jan. 1, 1891 . . . $57,289,004.04

RECEIVED IN 1891.

For Premiums	. . . $4,504,814.55	
For Interest and Rents.	3,215,354.27	
Profit and Loss .	81,310.18	
		7,801,479.00
		$65,093,575.04

DISBURSED IN 1891.

For claims by death and matured endowments . . .	$4,126,317.24	
Surplus returned to policy-holders .	1,161,209.56	
Lapsed and Surrendered Policies.	527,844.22	
TOTAL TO POLICY-HOLDERS, $5,815,371.02		
Commissions to Agents, Salaries, Medical Examiners' fees, Printing, Advertising, Legal, Real Estate, and all other Expenses .	. 777,039.74	
Taxes	291,767.40	
		6,885,778.16

BALANCE NET ASSETS, Dec. 31, 1891 . $58,207,794.88

SCHEDULE OF ASSETS.

Loans upon Real Estate, first lien	$16,417,373.87
Loans upon Stocks and Bonds . .	30,752.50
Premium Notes on Policies in force	1,869,873.30
Cost of Real Estate owned by the Co.	7,185,284.70
Cost of United States and other Bonds.	11,420,892.39
Cost of Bank and Railroad Stocks . .	405,685.25
Cash in Banks	1,150,865.85
Bills receivable	1,645.00
Balance due from Agents, secured	3,299.02
ADD	$58,207,794.88
Interest due and accrued	$411,349.26
Rents accrued . . .	7,110.65
Market value of stocks and bonds over cost . . .	128,487.70
Net deferred premiums	122,876.46
	1,530,185.07
GROSS ASSETS, Dec. 31, 1891	$59,738,179.95

LIABILITIES :

Amount required to re-insure all outstanding Policies, net, Company's standard . $52,705,312.00	
All other liabilities .	914,012.14
	53,673,324.14
SURPLUS by Company's Standard	$6,089,155.81
SURPLUS by State Reports will exceed .	6,650,000.00

Ratio of expenses of management to receipts in 1891 . . . . 9.98 per cent.

Policies in force Dec. 31, 1891, 61,794.	
Insuring	$155,043,055.00

JACOB L. GREENE, PRESIDENT.
JOHN M TAYLOR, VICE-PRES.
EDWARD M. BUNCE, SEC'Y.
D. H. WELLS, ACTUARY

PHILIP S. MILLER, General Agent.

1 WALL ST., NEW YORK.

168

HOME
INSURANCE COMPANY OF NEW YORK,

Office: No. 119 Broadway.

SEVENTY-SEVENTH SEMI-ANNUAL STATEMENT,
JANUARY, 1892.

SUMMARY OF ASSETS:

Cash in Banks,	$ 537,899 90
Real Estate,	1,544,938 96
Bonds and Mortgages, being first lien on Real Estate,	695,568 68
United States Stocks, (market value)	1,881,605 00
Bank, Trust Co., and Railroad Stocks and Bonds, (market value)	2,942,307 50
State and City Bonds, (market value),	871,737 39
Loans on Stocks, payable on demand,	347,735 00
Premiums uncollected and in hands of Agents,	497,708 62
Interest due and accrued on 1st January, 1892,	51,138 95
	$9,370,640 00

LIABILITIES:

Cash Capital,	$3,000,000 00
Reserve Premium Fund,	4,117,657 00
Reserve for Unpaid Losses and Claims,	962,592 74
Net Surplus,	1,290,390 26
	$9,370,640 00

DIRECTORS:

Levi P. Morton.
Henry A. Hurlbut.
William Sturgis,
John R. Ford,
William H. Townsend,
Oliver S. Carter.

Henry M. Taber,
Daniel A. Heald,
David H. McAlpin,
Andrew C. Armstrong,
Cornelius N. Bliss,
Edmund F. Holbrook.

John H. Washburn,
John H. Inman,
Walter H. Lewis.
Francis H. Leggett,
Benjamin Perkins,
Henry E. Beguelin,

George W. Smith,
George C. White,
Elbridge G. Snow,
George H. Hartford,
Henry F. Noyes,
Lucien C. Warner

DANIEL A. HEALD, President,

WILLIAM L. BIGELOW, } Secretaries.
THOMAS B. GREENE, }

JOHN H. WASHBURN, } Vice-Presidents.
ELBRIDGE G. SNOW, }

HENRY J. FERRIS, } Ass't Secretaries.
AREUNAH M. BURTIS, }

New York, January 12, 1892.

1851 ⇒‖⇐ 1893

The Phoenix Mutual ◎ ◎
Life Insurance Company ◎

◎ ◎ of Hartford, Conn..
after 41 years' of successful experience.
is one of the strongest, safest, and ◎
◎ best companies in the country. ◎
Contracts are brief, clear. and liberal,
containing all the valuable options of
modern life insurance. ◎ ◎

◎ ◎ ◎ H. Lindsley. General Agent.
◎ ◎ 189 Broadway. ◎ New York City

THE PIONEER COMPANY OF AMERICA

THOROUGH INSPECTIONS,

AND INSURANCE AGAINST LOSS OR DAMAGE
TO PROPERTY AND LOSS OF LIFE AND
INJURY TO PERSONS CAUSED BY · · ▫

STEAM BOILER EXPLOSIONS.

J. M. ALLEN, President.   GEN. W. B. FRANKLIN, Vice-President.
J. B. PIERCE, Secretary.   F. B. ALLEN, Second Vice-President.

BOARD OF DIRECTORS.

J. M. ALLEN, President.

FRANK W. CHENEY, Treas. Cheney Brothers Silk Manufacturing Co.

CHARLES M. BEACH, of Beach & Co.

DANIEL PHILLIPS, of Adams Express Co.

RICHARD W. H. JARVIS, President Colt's Fire Arms Manufacturing Co.

THOMAS O. ENDERS, President of the United States Bank.

LEVERETT BRAINARD, of The Case, Lockwood & Brainard Co.

GEN. WM. B. FRANKLIN, United States Commissioner to the Paris Exposition.

NELSON HOLLISTER, of State Bank, Hartford, Conn.

HON. HENRY C. ROBINSON, Attorney-at-Law, Hartford, Conn.

HON. FRANCIS B. COOLEY, of the National Exchange Bank, Hartford, Conn.

A. W. JILLSON, late Vice-President Phœnix Fire Insurance Co., Hartford, Conn.

EDMUND A. STEDMAN, Treasurer of the Fidelity Co., of Hartford, Conn.

GEORGE BURNHAM, Baldwin Locomotive Works, Philadelphia.

HON. NATHANIEL SHIPMAN, Judge U. S. Circuit Court.

C. C. KIMBALL, President Smyth Manufacturing Co., Hartford, Conn.

PHILIP CORBIN, of P. & F. Corbin, New Britain, Conn.

173

W. G. HITCHCOCK & CO.,

C OMMISSION
MERCHANTS,

453 AND 455 BROOME ST.,

NEW YORK.

SOLE AGENTS FOR

B. PRIESTLEY & CO.
SAMUEL COURTAULD & CO.
LYONS SILK AND TAPESTRY CO.

The Mercantile Agency,

R. G. Dun & Co.

314 & 316 Broadway,

New York.

EMERSON

1849.

EMERSON PIANO CO.'S NEW FACTORY, BOSTON.
Erected in 1890. The largest and most thoroughly equipped Piano Factory in America or Europe.

EMERSON PIANO CO.,

Warerooms, No. 116 Boylston St., Boston.

BRANCH STORES:

No. 92 Fifth Avenue, New York.   No. 218 Wabash Avenue, Chicago.

179

ARLINGTON ❖ MILLS,

LAWRENCE, MASS.

PRESIDENT,

ALBERT WINSLOW NICKERSON.

TREASURER,

WILLIAM WHITMAN.

CLERK,

WILLIAM P. ELLISON.

DIRECTORS,

ALBERT WINSLOW NICKERSON,

WILLIAM A. RUSSELL,   CHARLES C. BURR,

GEORGE A. NICKERSON,   WILLIAM WHITMAN.

RESIDENT AGENT,

ROBERT REDFORD.

SUPERINTENDENT OF WORSTED MILLS,

WILLIAM D. HARTSHORNE.

SUPERINTENDENT OF COTTON MILLS,

GEORGE E. TOWNE.

SELLING AGENTS,

HARDING, WHITMAN & CO.

TREASURER'S OFFICE,   . 78 CHAUNCY STREET, BOSTON.

NEW YORK SALESROOMS,   . 80 and 82 LEONARD STREET.

BOSTON SALESROOMS,   78 CHAUNCY STREET.

EDISON
Phonographs
⇒ FOR ∴ SALE ⇐

ADDRESS

North American Phonograph Co.,

EDISON BUILDING.

NEW ∴ YORK.

MASONIC TEMPLE BUILDING,

CHICAGO.

Cheney Brothers,

Silk Manufacturers,

New-York.

477 Broome St.

182

STRANGE & BROTHER,

✻

SILKS AND RIBBONS,

✻

96 and 98 Prince St.,

NEW YORK.

FALL · RIVER · LINE.

POSTAL TELEGRAPH BUILDING,
Broadway and Murray Street,
NEW YORK CITY.

189

IN AMERICA:

21,000 Telegraph Offices,

725,000 Miles of Wire.

EUROPEAN AGENCIES:

LONDON, - - - - No. 21, Royal Exchange, E. C.
LIVERPOOL, - - - - 25, Exchange Buildings.
BRISTOL, - - - - Backhall Chambers; and at
ANTWERP, ZURICH and GENOA.

CABLE SERVICE.

2 AMERICAN CABLES direct from NEW-YORK TO GREAT BRITAIN.

EXCLUSIVE CONNECTION WITH

4 ANGLO-AMERICAN TELEGRAPH CO'S CABLES.

1 DIRECT UNITED STATES CO'S CABLE.

WITH INDEPENDENT OFFICES AT

London, Paris, Edinburgh, Manchester, Newcastle, Glasgow,
Dundee, Bradford, Leith, Havre,

AND AGENCIES AT

Barcelona, Amsterdam and Trieste.

Direct Cable Connection with **France** and **Germany**, also with **Cuba, West Indies, Mexico, Bermuda, Nassau, and Central and South America.**

MESSAGES SENT TO ALL PARTS OF THE WORLD.

To insure the prompt and correct transmission of their messages, foreign correspondents should be instructed to mark them " via WESTERN UNION," for which indication no charge is made.

100

192

MANHATTAN TRUST COMPANY,

Corner Wall and Nassau Sts., NEW YORK CITY.

CAPITAL · · · · $1,000,000.

THE Company is authorized to act as Executor, Administrator, Guardian, Receiver, and Trustee ; as Fiscal and Transfer Agent, and as a Registrar of Stocks and Bonds. The Company offers exceptional facilities to Executors and Trustees of Estates, and to Religious and Benevolent Institutions, for the transaction of their business.

Deposits received subject to cheque at sight, payable through the New York Clearing House.

Liberal Rates of Interest Paid on Balances.

OFFICERS.

JOHN I. WATERBURY, President.

JOHN KEAN, Jr., Vice-President.   AMOS T. FRENCH, Second Vice-President.
R. B. GRINNELL, Asst. Treasurer.   C. H. SMITH, Assistant Secretary.

DIRECTORS, 1893.

FRANCIS ORMOND FRENCH	New York	JOHN KEAN, Jr.	..th, N. J
AUGUST BELMONT	New York	H. O. NORTHCOTE	London
C. C. BALDWIN	New York	L. D. RANDOLPH	New York
H. W. CANNON	New York	A. S. ROSENBAUM	New York
T. J. COOLIDGE, Jr	Boston	JAMES O. SHELDON	New York
R. J. CROSS	New York	SAMUEL R. SHIPLEY	Philadelphia
JOHN N. A. GRISWOLD	New York	CHARLES E. TAG	New York
JOHN R. FORD	New York	R. T. WILSON	New York
H. L. HIGGINSON	Boston	JOHN I. WATERBURY	New York

193

BLISS, FABYAN & CO.

32, 34 & 36 THOMAS AND

117 & 119 DUANE STREETS,

NEW-YORK.

BOSTON: 100 SUMMER STREET.
PHILA.: 1107 MARKET STREET.

G. H. MUMM & CO.

EXTRA DRY.

FAMOUS FOR ITS

EXCELLENCE, PURITY · · · ·

AND

NATURAL DRYNESS.

❖❘❦❖

"By chemical analysis the purest and most wholesome champagne."
R. Ogden Doremus M.D., LL.D., Professor of Chemistry, N. Y.

❖❘❦❖

Custom House statistics show that the importations in 1892 of G. H. MUMM & CO'S EXTRA DRY reached 75,880 cases, being more than one-fifth of the entire champagne importation, and over 9,000 cases more than of any other brand.

❖❘❦❖

FRED'K de BARY & CO., New York,

SOLE AGENTS.

DU VIVIER & CO'S Specialties.

Perrier Jouët
CHAMPAGNE.

FINEST SELECTION
OF
CLARETS & **B**URGUNDIES
IN THE U.S.

PERRIER JOUËT
Special

Gillé
Edac
Rye.

HINCKEL & WINCKLER
FRANKFORT A/M.
Rhine & Moselle
wines.

COATES & CO'S
ORIGINAL
PLYMOUTH
GIN.
DOUBLE DISTILLED,
UNSWEETENED.
PUREST & FINEST.
MOST WHOLESOME.

PARAGON
RYE
WHISKIES.

OVery Finest
LIVE **O**IL
A. BERUIE, — BORDEAUX.
Pronounced By Epicures,
"Unsurpassed."
DuVivier & Co., 22 Warren St. N.Y.

KINAHAN'S
LL

THE
CREAM
OF
IRISH WHISKY.

DU VIVIER & CO.

Bordeaux,   22 Warren Street, N. Y.

THE H. B. CLAFLIN COMPANY

White Goods,	Silks,
Laces and Embroideries,	Dress Goods, Flannels,
Hosiery, Notions,	Carpets, Cloaks,
Cloths, Shawls,	Suits and Furs.

PRINTS AND DOMESTICS.

CHURCH STREET,

WORTH STREET, AND WEST BROADWAY,

NEW-YORK.

Tefft, Weller & Co.,

Importers and Jobbers of

Dry Goods,

326, 328, 330 Broadway,

New York.

The House of Walter Baker & Co.

The oldest, and at the present time one of the largest industrial establishments in Boston, is that of WALTER BAKER & COMPANY, Manufacturers of Breakfast Cocoa, and other Cocoa and Chocolate Preparations. The extensive mills belonging to this house are situated on the Neponset River, partly in the Dorchester district of this city and partly in the town of Milton. The small mill in which the business was first begun, at the same place, in 1765, is said to be the first of its kind in the British Provinces of North America. The plant then established came into the possession of Dr. James Baker, in 1780, who was succeeded later by Walter Baker, his grandson, in whose name the business has since been conducted.

It is an extremely interesting fact, and one with scarcely a parallel, perhaps, in our industrial annals, that on the very spot where, more than a century and a quarter ago, the business of chocolate-making was first begun in this country, there has grown up one of the largest establishments of that kind in the world—an establishment which competes successfully for prizes in all the great industrial exhibitions in Europe and America, whose influence is felt in the great commercial centres, and whose prosperity promotes the welfare of men who labor under a tropical sun in the cultivation of one of the choicest fruits of the earth.

The chocolate-plant, known to botanists as *Theobroma cacao* (the first or generic word meaning "food of the gods"), flourishes only in hot climates, mostly within the fifteenth parallels of latitude. The cacao beans used by the manufacturers are procured mainly from South America, some of the West India Islands, Ceylon, Java, and certain parts of Africa.

The establishment of Walter Baker & Company, to which extensive additions have been made from time to time during the last fifty years, now comprises five large mills, equipped with all the latest and most improved machinery for the manufacture of cocoa and chocolate in a variety of forms and by the most approved methods. A large number of work-people are employed, and the total annual output reaches a very high figure. The high degree of perfection which this house has attained in its manufactured products is the result of long experience combined with an intelligent use of the new forces which are constantly being introduced to increase the power and improve the quality of production, and cheapen the cost to the consumer.

The full strength and the exquisite natural flavor of the raw material are preserved un-impaired in all of Walter Baker & Company's preparations; so that their products may truly be said to form the standard of purity and excellence. Their Breakfast Cocoa, in which a high degree of fineness is secured without any loss of brilliancy in color, can be used by students of the microscope and of chemistry, as a perfect type of the highest order of excellence in manufacture. They have always taken a decided stand against any and all chemically treated cocoas, and they believe that the large and increasing demand for their goods has proved that the consumer appreciates this decision.

New York Central
and Hudson River
⌒Railroad Company.

"America's⌒
A Greatest
Railroad"

Unsurpassed facilities for quick
and direct transportation over its
Four=Track line between New
York and all Western points.

Agencies in all the leading cities.

NATHAN GUILFORD, Gen'l Traffic Manager.
E. CLARK, Jr., Gen'l Freight Agent.
W. L. KINGMAN, Ass't Gen'l Freight Agent,
   Grand Central Station, New York.

R. L. CRAWFORD, Gen'l Eastern Freight Agent,
413 Broadway, New York.

www.ingramcontent.com/pod-product-compliance
Lightning Source LLC
Chambersburg PA
CBHW030823270326
41928CB00007B/874